· BRET EASTON ELLIS'S

American Psycho

A READER'S GUIDE

JULIAN MURPHET

CONTINUUM | NEW YORK | LONDON

2002

The Continuum International Publishing Group Inc
370 Lexington Avenue, New York, NY 10017

The Continuum International Publishing Group Ltd
The Tower Building, 11 York Road, London SE1 7NX

www.continuumbooks.com

Printed in the United States of America

Library of Congress Cataloging-in-Publication Data

Murphet, Julian.
    Bret Easton Ellis's American Psycho : a reader's guide / Julian
Murphet.
        p. cm. — (Continuum contemporaries)
    Includes bibliographical references (p.   ).
    ISBN 0-8264-5245-0 (pbk. : alk. paper)
    1. Ellis, Bret Easton. American psycho. 2. Serial murderers in
literature. 3. Violence in literature.   I. Title. II. Series.
PS3555.L5937 A836 2002
813'.54—dc21   2001047384

Contents

for Olivia
who lived it

Acknowledgments

Thanks to Dominic Oliver, Daniel Hedley and Katy Mullin, for reading some of it; to St. John's College, Oxford, for letting me do it; and to Pam Thurschwell for getting me the gig. And thanks to Bret Easton Ellis for writing the book in the first place.

The Novelist

T he eldest of three children raised in a well-heeled household in the affluent suburbs of Los Angeles, Bret Easton Ellis was born to a mother who loved reading and a heavy-drinking father in the real estate industry. His parents separated unamicably while Ellis was a boy and though he was raised by his mother, his father continued to exert a mostly negative influence on the future writer's life. "He was", says Ellis, "the sort of person who was completely obsessed with status and about wearing the right suits and owning a certain kind of car and staying at a certain kind of hotel and eating in a certain kind of restaurant regardless of whether these things gave him pleasure or not."[1] Avatars of this figure appear in most of the novels, fathers who are as culpably implicated in the shallow consumerism of the culture as their cynical sons and daughters. Ellis is grudging and unforthcoming about his father in interview, but there can be little question that his failure as a bourgeois *paterfamilias*, his neglect and infantile obsession with status and style, helped shape the preoccupying themes of the author; indeed, *American Psycho* itself has been described by Ellis as "my send off to my dad, my way of saying, 'I'm going to escape your grasp somehow'. "

Introduced to Ernest Hemingway by his mother, Ellis has consistently cited *The Sun Also Rises* (*Fiesta*) as one of his most important literary influences. Hemingway's sparse and uninflected prose style has had a strong bearing on the stylistic texture of Ellis's books, which are uniformly written in a signature affectless, flattened prose. It is a style shaped also by his exposure, in a class on "The Personal Essay" at his private high school, Buckley, to the New Journalism of Tom Wolfe, Truman Capote, and especially Joan Didion. Didion's ongoing concern, in fiction and non-fiction alike, with the flattening of human subjectivity, the ambience of 'non-places' such as highways, hotel rooms, lobbies and airports, the erasure of ethics in contemporary society, and above all the stripping away of literary ostentation from her prose style, have all been carried on loyally throughout Ellis's career. Her fastidious reinvention of the 'literary sentence' as close to journalistic objectivity as possible, free from rhetoric, colour, sentiment and jejune philosophizing, was one of post-War America's most important literary developments; it persists as an ideal in all of Ellis's fiction.

At Bennington College in Vermont (fictionalized as 'Camden' in all of his works), Ellis made a place for himself in the monied artistic student set, and began producing written work for credit in a writing workshop under teacher Joe McGinniss. This work gradually evolved into the manuscript of his first novel, *Less Than Zero*, which was published in 1985 while Ellis was still enrolled at college, aged twenty-one. The novel (dedicated to McGinniss) describes a meandering Christmas break spent by its narrator, Clay, back home in Los Angeles away from Camden College. His experiences veer between banal trips to the mall and shocking exposure to snuff films, heroin dealing and his best friend's prostitution. The novel's consistent feature is the tone and style of its presentation, which ensures that a bland list of freeway names and the narration of a confrontation with a pimp are delivered in precisely the same register: blank, unaffected, cool, and 'non-literary'. Whether this unity of tone means simply that Clay is unable to distinguish between mutual masturbation with his girlfriend and lunch with his father, or that the quality of experience itself has been devalued by a consumerist culture, Ellis refuses to give his readers pleasure through stylistic grace. Even more so than in Didion, there is a marked aversion here from simile, metaphor, symbol and allegory, as though such devices were ill-suited to a generation reared on television and the spoils of overconsumption; rather, everything is immediate, particular, and denied any sense of connection with everything else. 'People are afraid to merge' are the first words of the novel; and even the sentences tend towards separation and parataxis.

The runaway commercial success of *Less Than Zero* was probably the single most significant event of Ellis's literary career. Although there was no initial media curiosity driving *Less Than Zero* into the national spotlight, as there would be for his later works, a word-of-mouth campaign produced large sales, and soon forced the young author and his work into 'representative' status for his entire generation. Nothing of this sort had happened since J. D. Salinger's *The Catcher in the Rye* had ignited a young generation's imagination more than thirty years earlier; and Salinger had strategically vanished from public view. As sales of his novel climbed, Ellis was confronted with the daunting prospect of being a media celebrity, a spokesman, a prophet, at an age when most young writers are struggling for ideas and the first shreds of recognition. He also found overnight wealth, an income comparable to those of the stockbrokers, bankers and insurance men which many of his classmates at Bennington were becoming. This would be a pivotal factor in his production of *American Psycho*. As Ellis has said, "So I moved to

New York—this is an awful thing to say—as a very successful young man. I made an enormous amount of money and I moved to Manhattan and I sort of got sucked up into this whole yuppie-mania that was going on at the time and I think in a lot of ways, working on *American Psycho* was my way of fighting against myself slipping into a certain kind of lifestyle."

Meanwhile, however, Ellis had also managed to put together a follow-up novel set on the fictional environs of Camden, called *The Rules of Attraction* (1987). This campus novel, completed during his final year at Bennington, treats the experiences of several confused and interconnected students, each of whom has a first person voice in the novel. Although Ellis himself has expressed a particular fondness and partiality towards this novel, it was a commercial disappointment, and is in many ways his least successful book aesthetically as well. Lacking the consistency of voice of *Less Than Zero*, *American Psycho* and *Glamorama* (1997), and less boldly satirical than *The Informers* (1994), *Rules* is haunted by a sneaking mawkishness and sentimentality—nowhere evident as such—which make it feel less mature and poised than his first novel. Ellis obviously felt deeply attached to several of his characters here, a fact which is borne out in the reappearance of several of them in later works, and this emotional investment cuts against the venomous tone of much of the material, which in effect wants to show that Camden and the East are not the easy escape routes that *Less Than Zero* had made them appear to be.

What *Rules* did establish, however, was a roster of characters who would then appear from novel to novel; names from *Less Than Zero* pop up here, and almost all of these characters would appear later in *American Psycho*, *The Informers*, and *Glamorama*. This ongoing elaboration of Ellis's fictional *milieu* is one of the keys to his ambitions as a writer. Unlike some of his contemporaries, Ellis has deliberately kept to a very minimalist palette, using the reiteration of names (like themes and ideas) to underscore his larger satiric concerns: the identity, indifference, and repetition of human character. Although each novel has, in a sense, accommodated a 'larger' social frame than the previous one (home, college, city, the world of fashion), this insistence on the same names, faces and above all the same language style, drives home the point for his long-term readers that, fundamentally, nothing really changes from scale to scale. "My point being", he says, "that the worlds of *Less Than Zero* and *Glamorama* aren't really that much different. After fourteen years I've changed in some ways but the fictive universe I'm creating really hasn't. The concerns are the same, the themes are the same, the tonality of the writing is the same." At the high end of the literary spectrum in America we may think of William Faulkner; at the lower end perhaps Stephen King—in either case, a serious concern for the development of an integrated fictional universe peopled by increasingly 'epic' characters, knows its satiric comeuppance and deflation in the singularly unepical, monodimensional 'names' of Ellis's texts, which may or may not refer to the 'same' characters. They are all much the same anyway.

It was in the period surrounding the pre-publication, cancellation and publication of *American Psycho* (1991) that Ellis truly entered center-stage as America's most notorious and 'dangerous' mainstream writer. The episode itself will be treated at greater length in Chapter 3; suffice it to say here that the leaking of certain of the book's most disturbing passages to the media, and the decision by the editorial board at Simon & Schuster to drop it on the basis of these passages' excruciating violence against women, provoked the most animated controversy on America's literary scene since *Lolita*. Sexual violence had loomed large in the culture wars gripping America at the time, and although what happened was not a case of censorship by any stretch of the imagination, nevertheless it appeared that Simon & Schuster's hasty decision constituted either a violation of free speech, or a blow in favour of feminist concerns about the exploitation of women. Neither is in fact the case, as we shall see. However, the sheer degree of media noise surrounding this episode forever branded Ellis with the cultural notoriety he now both relishes and resists. Any press is good press, we may say, and anyone caring to plough through editions of *The New York Times* over this period will get a good idea of the amount of space being devoted to this episode, if not to the novel itself.[2] Ellis has been both victim and beneficiary of this attention; readers may unfortunately have taken easy refuge in media banality, rather than actually read the work; but buyers aplenty there have certainly been.

The conditions of production of the manuscript itself are if anything more interesting. Ellis's move to New York, and his immersion in the 'yuppie lifestyle' of conspicuous consumption, status, and greed, presented the young writer with a dilemma. On the one hand, he was attracted to the glamour of the slick Manhattan inhabited by his friends; on the other, he was a writer who had built his brief but already substantial career to date on excoriating this very 'lifestyle' with acid satire. He wanted to regard the life of the Wall Street trader as mere 'material' on which to go to work as a corruscating satiric author, but he was so close to his subject matter, immersing himself so deeply in the life, that the danger of becoming his own object of contempt was great. Thus, an inevitable psychological crisis took root in the imaginative humus of the work itself; Ellis's torsion, his internal vacillation between being and hating the yuppie he was constructing as Patrick Bateman, manifested itself as one long, excruciating period of depression, which then emanated in the bleakness, horror and 'insanity' of the text. Three years spent building up a character without a character, without moral tissue, left Ellis exhausted and mentally shaken; but with a typescript that would become a sensation.

The temptation to ascribe the gruesome violence of the text, its often nauseating and explicit detail, to Ellis's mental state, however, must be firmly resisted. It has been too easy for moralistic critics of the novel to latch on to these passages (which constitute less than ten percent of the text) as instances of Ellis's own misogynistic bile and disturbed imagination. In fact, these are some of the most factual and research-based sections of the novel—literally the furthest from Ellis's own imagination. As he has said:

The research that I did was only to inform the murder sequences because I really had no idea where to go with that. These were sequences, four or five of them scattered throughout the book, that I left blank and didn't work on until the book was completed; then I went back and filled those scenes in. I didn't really want to write them, but I knew they had to be there. So I read a lot of books about serial killers and picked up details from that and then I had a friend who introduced me to someone who could get me criminology textbooks from the FBI that really went into graphic detail about certain motifs in the actual murders committed by serial killers and detailed accounts of what serial killers did to bodies, what they did to people they murdered, especially sex killings. That's why I did the research, because I couldn't really have made this up.

So, the unsettling truth is that, far from being the sick and perverted rantings of a disturbed young man, these sections of *American Psycho* are based on actual cases of serial killers. Of course, the details are packaged in a very particular style, as we shall see in the following chapter; but one of the effects of this style is that it makes us feel the very same resistance to reading these episodes that Ellis mentions feeling when composing them.

American Psycho was followed three years later by what appears in comparison to be a much slighter work, which returns to his homeground of Los Angeles after the previous novels' relocation to the East. *The Informers* is, however, if anything the most accomplished text of Ellis's career, in terms of sheer technical and stylistic discipline and thematic consistency. Less a novel than a series of thirteen interconnected short stories, this work probes expertly, with as many narrators as chapters, the key and recurrent concerns of Ellis's fictional *ouevre*: the absence of innocence, the hollowness of character, lack of connection, the arrogance, indifference, apathy and sheer waste of so much of white, middle-class America. 'Imagine a blind person dreaming' is the central motto of the book, just as 'people are afraid to merge' and 'disappear here' had been of *Less Than Zero* and 'abandon hope' and 'this is not an exit' were of *American Psycho*. Ellis is adept at producing resonant phrases and locating them in the novel as signatures of his organizing presence. But even if *The Informers* had been a more disciplined effort, and less driven by sensational elements than *American Psycho*, precisely this 'taming' of his talents inevitably disappointed a reading and commenting public now expecting the outrageous from Ellis. In fact, the most disturbing section of the book, which concerns a community of Republican-voting vampires, was toned down and made much more palatable during the editing stage, to avoid exploiting the kind of reputation Ellis had made for himself.

In 1997, Ellis released his much-anticipated long novel, *Glamorama*. This work was distinguished from the rest of his fiction, not only by an international setting worthy of a spy novel (New York, London, Paris, Milan), but also by an unprecedented amount of narrative impetus. Ellis had up to this point worked almost exclusively within a non-narrative mode of literary construction, prefering the effect of the work to emerge from the mounting of episode upon disjointed episode, with no apparent links or story to hold the whole edifice together. Here, on the other hand, is a story of international nihilistic terrorism working under the apparently harmless face of *haute couture* modeling, celebrity, and the fashion industry. Like the previous works, it too is presented in the voice of a vapid protagonist who has no real idea about politics or the running of the world, and who speaks predominantly in direct quotations from pop songs; but in *Glamorama* this character gradually becomes aware of what he does not know. As Victor Ward/Johnson is told by another character, "it's what you don't know that matters most," and for the first time in an Ellis novel, this otherwise unstated premis of his literary satire is directly stated and negotiated through Victor's gradual realization of a narrative pattern that envelops him. Of course, nothing is straightforward in this fiction, and Victor (and we) can only approach the existence of this hidden narrative order (assassination plots, Presidential candidacy, replicants) through the bizarre frame of several competing 'film crews' who haunt the novel, mediating between Victor and his various storylines, giving him advice, worrying about his performance; and of course the story itself is so video-game-like and preposterous as to call itself into question whenever it comes into view.

It is most likely that Ellis will continue in the direction marked out by *Glamorama* with subsequent work (his next novel promises to be set in Washington DC among the political elite): further narrative sophistication, blending with his preoccupying interest in the shallowness and stupidity of the general culture of America. What is more, the apparent narrowness of this overriding thematic interest, which has significantly limited the sales of Ellis's novels abroad and in translation, looks like becoming less of an issue the more Americanization, McDonaldsization and a general law of cultural equivalence comes to dominate most of the world under the banner of 'globalization'. Intuitively, as an eighteen-year-old writing student in the early 1980s, Ellis had latched on to one of the most salient and pressing cultural topics of our time, and has since made it into his most abiding fictional subject: the eradication of difference, subjectivity, free will and discrimination under a regime of absolute commercialization. As one of the white, wealthy and middle-class characters reflects in *The Informers*, "I realized that no matter where I am it's always the same. Camden, New York, LA, Palm Springs—it really doesn't seem to matter. Maybe this should be disturbing but it's really not. I find it kind of comforting."[3] *Glamorama* extends this leveling of space to a European canvas as well. To the extent that, as tourists, consumers and commuters, this is the lived experience of more and more of those who belong to the world's dominant group, Ellis's fictional material looks like becoming increasingly relevant as satire. If we call Ellis a 'postmodern' author, we probably mean this above all; this flattening and erasure of the texture of his world, manifest above all in the flatness and affectlessness of his prose style, to which we are meant to respond with a kind of cool outrage.

On the other hand, Ellis's stature as a satirist needs to be properly gauged here. The best kind of satirist, be it a Swift, a Juvenal, or an Orwell, certainly generates most of his effects by heaping contempt on whatever social vice or folly is under the scalpel; but he will not tend to frame his critique within the very idiom he sees as being symptomatic of the vice or folly in question. This is the high-risk gamble of Ellis's style, his decision always to remain in the first person voice of the character who is (with all he represents) the object of the author's scorn. This is problematic because classic satire always relies on some existing moral normativity against which to evaluate the social corruption or decadence it condemns; and, no doubt, Ellis too has some such ethico-political touchstone in mind when he settles down to excoriate his various drug-addled students, yuppies and celebrities. However, by remaining strictly within the very voice of his object of censure, Ellis can only be satirical by resorting to excesses of stupidity and hollowness in his own prose, thereby obviating the possibility of offering even the outline of another vision. Alexander Pope, on the contrary, scorned the 'dunces' of his age in an idiom whose supple perfectionism stood always as a guarantee of the very moral order put at risk by rampant idiocy. Ellis writes as the one-eyed man in the Kingdom of the Blind, who savagely affects the voice of the blind to echo their blindness back at them. His viciousness with his objects of ridicule is often very amusing, but it is amusing in the way the cruelest jokes are. Satire without any clear idea of a better moral and political universe is just bitter invective, and Ellis could often be accused of mere biliousness. So what does Ellis believe in?

According to his own testimony, he has never voted, and feels in general "rather apolitical." This is not surprising, although there are more than a few indictments of Republicanism in the novels (as complicitous with psychotic yupppies and vampires). Ellis does not have a political intelligence; though he does have a proto-political vision, and wishes to lodge a series of complaints against what a certain class and a certain Party have done to America in the name of free enterprise and the unchecked profit motive. He remains unable, however, to articulate these complaints within a discourse favourable towards any sort of social project. The silly pastiche of 'terrorism' in *Glamorama* is a clear giveaway here. Presumably, then, his moral idea stems not from a faith in the future, but is inherited from a previously existing state of affairs, which he remembers, even if in stereotyped form, from a 'golden age' in the not-too-distant past. My sense is that most of the values Ellis actually embraces in his fiction (and we can usually read these only negatively, against the grain of the narrating voice) inhered in a very brief period of the cultural past — in the period known as the punk movement, defined above all by a nihilistic contempt for established middle-class conformity, sartorial menace, and loud metallic noise; a concerted *épater le bourgeois* by urban youth. I feel that, like his comrade-in-arms, the writer Dennis Cooper, Ellis has kept the spirit of punk alive, albeit from within the well-manicured, yuppified exterior of a member of the MTV generation.

However, his most sensitive critic, Elizabeth Young, feels that nostalgia in Ellis goes much further back, to a pre-punk suburban security of nuclear families, strong moral codes and clearly defined gender roles:

The faults Ellis perceives in contemporary culture come from an old-fashioned, straightforwardly moralistic reading of it. . . . Ellis's vision is conformist and conventional. . . . He is denunciatory, a supporter of the status quo and in relation to this it is ironic to what a large extent he has been depicted as some sort of literary tearaway.[4]

I do think rhetoric has got the better of Young here. There is scant evidence in the texts themselves that Ellis is a 'supporter of the status quo', however mesmerized his narrators appear to be by it. And while it is true that, in interview, Ellis claims to be 'apolitical', not to vote, and believes that a character such as Patrick Bateman represents something not historical but fundamental to human nature (a very conservative claim), there is so much more of the spirit, audacity and Nietzschean post-morality of the punk movement to Ellis's novels than the saccharine '1950s' conformism to which Young is clearly pointing. Ellis the writer, or 'Ellis' the body of texts, is much more interesting and complex than Ellis the interviewee (as is always the case of any important writer, or we should not need literature at all!), that we would do better to attend to the complex infrastructure of values that occasionally gleams through the banality and monotony of the narrating voice of the fiction. More often than not, those values are 'denunciatory,' to be sure, but much more in the style of a Johhny Rotten than a Billy Graham. We may wonder how many punks ever chose to vote.

· **2**

The Novel

"It seemed like a nice neighborhood to have bad habits in."
RAYMOND CHANDLER

"Thus the most general abstractions commonly appear where there is the highest concrete development, where one feature appears to be shared by many, and to be common to all."
KARL MARX

The forbidding inscription over Hell's Gate in *The Inferno* — 'abandon all hope ye that enter' — is met by Dante with a plea to Vergil on the subject of the words: 'Master, their meaning to me is hard.' Bret Easton Ellis's most notorious novel opens with the same admonition, but there is no authorial presence here to make the point that the meaning of the words in the ensuing Hell are 'hard', nor is there any benign Vergil to clarify their significance for us. We are in these words up to our eyes and ears, with no navigator or reassuring narrator beyond the 'psycho' of the title; and much of the controversy surrounding the book stemmed from this lack of a reliable guide. Making meaning of the various inscriptions, the layers and layers of language which make up the novel, was a task made deceptively facile for some readers by the sheer visceral force of the work's most infamous passages. The various murders and acts of torture could be seized upon as effectively the *only* content worth scrutinizing; and considered apart from the rest of the book, they are so objectionable that the 'meaning' of the novel could be reduced to sensationalist exploitation. However, *American Psycho* is a perversely unified text, and the rest of the book—a good ninety percent of it—is a carefully considered foil to the violence. Some of the emptiest dialogue ever committed to print; ghastly, endless descriptions of home electronics and men's grooming products, apparently distilled from actual sales catalogues; characters so undefined and interchangeable that even *they* habitually confuse each others' identity; and a central narrating voice which seems unable and unwilling to raise itself above the literary distinction of an inflight magazine: all this material, so unpropitious, must also be made to mean. If Ellis wants to bore us, he must have a reason. What is required, if the work is to be taken as seriously as Dante's warning tells us it wants to be, is some analytic procedure able to tease apart and understand Ellis's aesthetics of boredom. I want to do so by way of a progressive stylistic analysis, to demonstrate that one of the most inconsistent narrative voices in contemporary fiction means more than the white noise it appears to be.

THE STYLES OF AMERICAN PSYCHO

Grammatically, as is the rule with all of Ellis's works, the book is presented almost uniformly in a first person, present tense voice in the indicative mood. This is fundamental to Ellis's effects of boredom. An unmodulated voice of this sort necessarily creates enormous resistance in the reader's mind, and the monotonous consistency of Bateman's monologue dispells most of our expectations of 'style' from this reading experience. It is a provocative and mocking deflation of our hopes that literature should explore the best and most meaningful potentialities of our language. Our total immersion in the first person also promotes the narrating 'I' of the text to an unchallangeable ascendancy which, since it is in the present tense, strays into solipsism; albeit a solipsism populated by the signs and brand-names of consumer society. Although many texts, including some great American ones such as Mark Twain's *The Adventures of Huckleberry Finn* and Saul Bellow's *The Adventures of Augie March*, are written in the first person, none so deliberately explores the unadventurousness of that voice as *American Psycho*. Where a first person voice does not commit itself to breaking out of its habitual expressions and launching upon some experiential river or highway, but on the contrary fixes itself to habit with a ferocious determination, the effect is quite the opposite from the usual literary conception of a 'self'. Rather, what the voice gives us is a kind of *non-self*, a self defined not by freedom and the open horizon of the undetermined, but by repetition and tunnel vision. This is in one sense the design of Ellis's novel, an interminable monologue of the non-self, which is, at some hypothetical socio-psychological limit, the lived 'self' of everyday life in contemporary America.

Bateman's monologue can thus be seen as a 'corrective' to literary escapism. Rather than offer us a better vision of the individual in modern society by exposing his narrative voice to a variegated experience from which it duly learns the meaning of the human, Ellis gives us instead the unreflexive repetition and monomania of a voice that has not escaped the cocoon of its own routine, and enacts the inhumanity of pure habit. We readers are not offered the consolations of the 'novel' as such; here, nothing is *new*, all is prescribed, and the shape, texture and depth of the voice does not

alter. Its monotony is the whir and hum of everyday life itself,
which, despite all the rotations of fashion, fundamentally repeats its
own elements and structures in a seamless procession of the same.
And this is where the virtually unbroken present tense secures its
most powerful hold over the meaning of the work as well. Every
narrated instant (violence aside) is presented in the flat immediacy
of the present, as though it has already been lived. What might in
some other use of this tense have been a dizzying revolution of new
perceptions and affections, is exchanged stylistically for the numb
conviction that past and future have both collapsed into a point
without dimension or dynamism, which the voice occupies indiffer-
ently — the 'end of history' as Hell.

Tonally, the voice is packaged into a cynical and snobbish acer-
bity, which is always ready to draw the worst conclusions and make
the least generous concessions to anything but its own interests:

Cheryl, this dumpy chick who is in love with me, sits at her desk up front
signing people in, reading one of the gossip columns in the *Post*, and she
brightens up noticeably when she sees me approaching. She says hello but
I move past her quickly, barely registering her presence since there's no
line at the Stairmaster, for which ususally one has to wait twenty minutes.
With the Stairmaster you work the body's largest muscle group (between
the pelvis and knees) and you can end up burning more calories per
minute than by doing any other aerobic activity, except maybe Nordic
skiing. (p. 68)

While unflattering adjectives ('dumpy') generally flock to the other
figures in its range, the voice vainly assumes these figures' sponta-
neous genuflection in its vicinity. Patrick Bateman, who is the
accumulated identity of this kind of cynical egotism, is also always
ready with a preposterous exercise in pedantic 'information', evidence of his mastery over the facts and products which make him

so desireable. Here it is the pointless aside on the Stairmaster, but elsewhere, at much greater length, it is generally the finer points of male sartorial etiquette and home stereo equipment which animate Bateman's pedantic streak.

It is at these moments of pure information, however, that the voice tends to abandon its tone altogether and fold back into the undifferentiated discourse of trade copy and promotional literature. Whatever tonal portrait we may have been able to sketch of Bateman (selfish, arrogant, unfeeling), dissipates the minute he launches into a description of the contents of his apartment; or tells us in excruciating detail about his morning toilet:

One should use an alcohol-free antibacterial toner with a water-moistened cotton ball to normalize the skin. Applying a moisturizer is the final step. Splash on water before applying an emollient lotion to soften the skin and seal in the moisture. Next apply Gel Appaisant, also made by Pour Hommes, which is an excellent, soothing skin lotion. If the face seems dry and flaky—which makes it look dull and older—use a clarifying lotion that removes flakes and uncovers fine skin (it can also make your tan look darker). (p. 27)

Notice that the first person (with which this enormous five-page paragraph begins) has given way to a third person/second person singluar in the imperative mood, straight from the pages of an instruction manual or advice column. The general has here absorbed the particular to such an extent that all vestiges of 'Patrick' have vanished in the veneer of promotion. Also notice the glaring product placement, a feature of the book generally, with its excessive displays of Armani, Ralph Lauren and others. These factors are not unrelated, and 'Armani' and 'Oliver Peoples' are in some sense more stable and identifiable 'characters' in the text than Bateman himself (in the later *Glamorama*, 'Calvin Klein' sometimes refers to the person, sometimes to the designer label). The adjectives used for Gel Appaisant ('excellent, soothing') are so much more lively and human than those used for the people in the text.

In the following passage, the people are invisible, swallowed by the various products they wear:

> I count three silk-crepe ties, one Versace silk-satin woven tie, two silk foulard ties, one silk Kenzo, two silk jacquard ties. The fragrances of Xeryus and Tuscany and Armani and Obsession and Polo and Grey Flannel and even Antaeus mingle, wafting into each other, rising from the suits and into the air, forming their own mixture: a cold, sickening perfume. (p. 110)

Devoid of even the hint of a human being, this rich and fascinated description luxuriates in the allure of a kind of commercial nominalism — everything has its proper name — which we will want to address more fully later under the rubric of *reification*.

Next, however, there is the business of dialogue, which interrupts the monologue with the voices of others, potentially destabilising the solipsism of the discourse; though in fact this very rarely happens. By and large the dialogue of the novel is written as light satire, the inanity of the various conversations — mostly about restaurant bookings and dress style — underpinned by the clear lack of distinction between one voice and another. The satire of vapidity and the confusions of conference calling is pushed to its limit in a very late chapter, "Another Night", a section of which endless scene occurs as follows:

> I get back on the other line.
>
> "Bateman, I know this sounds like an impossibility", McDermott says. "But the void is actually widening."
>
> "I am not into Mexican", Van Patten states.
>
> "But wait, we're not having Mexican are we?" I say. "Am I confused? Aren't we going to Zeus Bar?"

"No, moron", McDermott spits. "We couldn't get into Zeus Bar. Kaktus. Kaktus at nine."

"But I don't want Mexican", Van Patten says.

"But you, Van Patten, made the reservation", McDermott hollers.

"I don't either", I say suddenly. "Why Mexican?"

"It's not *Mexican* Mexican", McDermott says, exasperated. "It's something called nouvelle Mexicana, tapas, or some other south of the border thing. Something like that. Hold on. My call waiting." (pp. 320–21)

And so on and on, the endless inane chatter never finally resolving anything; its monosyllables accented only by the brand names, restaurant names and cuisine styles which promise some moment of future consumption. Are the voices actually distinguishable? Or are they not mere prehensile extensions of a single, interminable inner monologue, caught in a clumsy hesitation over where to go, what to do? Ellis makes the point here that the technology of conference calling itself contributes to the abstraction of the voices from any determinable context; calls wait, lines cross, reservations are made and unmade, all in the same empty space. Chapters such as the various "Harrys", "Yale Club" and "Another Night" are dominated by this light satiric style of dialogue.

However, when Bateman is engaged in dialogue with a woman, generally in restaurant scenes, a different kind of ambience surrounds the exchanges. Rather than satiric blankness, there is generally a more venomous tone to the side Bateman invariably takes against his female interlocutors. At lunch with his hapless girlfriend Evelyn, Bateman can scarcely tolerate the blandness of her language, which he represents for us thus:

". . . Tandoori chicken and foie gras, and lots of jazz, and he adored the Savoy, but shad roe, the colors were gorgeous, aloe, shell, citrus, Morgan Stanley . . ."

I clasp my hands back where they were, pressing even tighter. Once again hunger overtakes me and so humming loudly to myself I reach again for the spoon, but it's hopeless: Evelyn's voice is at a particular pitch that cannot be ignored. . . .

"I have no idea who Gregory is. You do know that, right?"

Evelyn puts her spoon down delicately next to the plate of pudding and looks into my eyes. "Mr. Bateman, I really like you. I *adore* your sense of humor." She gives my hand a soft squeeze and laughs, actually *says*, "Ha-ha-ha . . .", but she's serious, not joking. Evelyn really *is* paying me a compliment. She *does* admire my sense of humor. (p. 122)

We of course, privy to Bateman's utter removal from the conversation/monologue, can only concur with his astonishment. Evelyn's language is presented through the filter of Bateman's as mere list-making: ". . . Groton, Lawrenceville, Milton, Exeter, Kent, Sain Paul's, Hotchkiss, Andover, Milton, Choate . . . oops, already said Milton . . ." (p. 123). The intervening verbs and presiding intentionality are lost; Bateman hears only an endless succession of proper names behind which no organizing consciousness could exist. Similarly, Evelyn sees nothing in Patrick but an embodied list of all the usual entries in the singles columns: attractive, single, good sense of humor, professional, etc. Men and women do not so much talk to each other here as pile up meaningless, irreconcilable lists on dishes garnished with indifference.

On a date with another girl whose discourse is even less appealing to him, Bateman ends up gibbering to himself with his own list:

J&B I am thinking. Glass of J&B in my right hand I am thinking. Hand I am thinking. Charivari. Shirt from Charivari. Fusilli I am thinking. Jami Gertz I am thinking. I would like to fuck Jami Gertz I am thinking. Porsche 911. A Sharpei I am thinking. I would like to own a Sharpei. I am twenty-six years old I am thinking. I will be twenty-seven next year. A Valium. I would like a Valium. No, two Valium I am thinking. Cellular phone I am thinking. (pp. 80–1)

Non sequiturs such as these dominate the scenes of inter-sexual conversation (although: remember the Sharpei), because in Bateman's text, *there is no sexual relation.* Jacques Lacan coined this phrase to indicate a constitutive antagonism between men and women which the conventions and rituals of love strive to erase. In *American Psycho* there is no love, and the antagonism remains absolute. That is to say, men and women in this textual world exist on parallel, untouching and opposed planes of reality; each sex satisfies for the other only preconceived and fixed expectations, within a general campaign of seige and domination. What do the girls want? "They want a hardbody who can take them to Le Cirque twice a week, get them into Nell's on a regular basis. Or maybe a close personal friend of Donald Trump." (p. 54) And a 'good personality' in a woman "consists of a chick who has a little hardbody and who will satisfy all sexual demands without being too slutty about things and who will essentially keep her dumb fucking mouth *shut.*" (p. 91). With the lines of demarcation drawn so inexorably, there can be no relation or dialogue. A 'relationship' in this world where everybody sleeps with everybody anyway, is a cipher which may or may not turn into a 'wedding' — another cipher, only with many more products to wear and consume. Unthinkable terms include 'marriage' and 'children' (the sight of a breast-feeding mother 'awakens something awful' in Bateman, p. 297). As he remarks of his own relationship with Evelyn, in a rather unconvincing moment of self-awareness, it is no more than "an isolation ward that serves only to expose my own severely impaired capacity to feel." (p. 343)

Bateman's conversations with working-class and ethnically differentiated characters are grotesquely overstated episodes in what can only be described as Patrick's class and race war against everything that does not resemble him. This will be discussed more fully when we analyse the politics of the work in general, but it is worth bearing

in mind the sickly comic scene in the Chinese dry cleaners, where
Bateman, complaining about the persistence of gory blood-stains on
his Soprani sheets, encounters a tirade of suspicious shrieking.

"Two things," I say, talking over her. "One. You can't bleach a Soprani.
Out of the question. Two"—and then louder, still over her—"*two*, I
can only get these sheets in Santa Fe. These are very expensive sheets
and I *really* need them clean. . . ." But she's still talking and I'm nodding
as if I understand her gibberish, then I break into a smile and lean right
into her face. "If-you-don't-shut-your-fucking-mouth-I-will-kill-you-are-you-
understanding-me?" (p. 82)

The Chinese woman's speech receives no notation, apart from the
repeated words 'gibberish' and 'jabbering', while Patrick's speech is
carefully detailed, and armed with stage directions. Bateman has no
means (or will) at his disposal for the rendering of 'other' speech.
The comedy of this scene derives in part from this utter inequality
of register in the text, in part from the disparity between the
woman's hysterical concern about the blood and Bateman's transformation of it into a complaint about the service, and in part from
Patrick's ever-escalating fury and desperation at his actual useless-
ness.

    This last point suggests an important way to read the voice of the
book: read against what Bateman actually manages to do (apart from
the violence, of which more later), the arrogant confidence of the
voice must be seen as a smokescreen masking risible ineffectuality.
Bateman is unable to reserve seats in Dorsia, unable to handle the
elusive Fisher account, unable to hire a new video, unable to hang
his David Onica the right way up, unable to be recognized by
anyone outside his immediate circle of friends, unable to strangle
Carruthers, unable to retain control over Paul Owen's apartment,
and so on. His ineffectuality as a central protagonist is extraordinary.

What he is able to do, with decreasing success, consists mainly of upholding his physical and public appearance through meticulous discipline, cliché and props. It is in this regard that his language of pedantry comes to mean so much — as pure compensation for the lack of any actual achievement. Bateman very precisely *does nothing*; but his control over certain kinds of information and 'taste' asssumes the importance for him of a kind of action. His psychosis as such has less to do with his violence than it does with the 'slippage' of his meticulously maintained 'mask of sanity' (p. 279), a breakdown in his ability to cover his nothingness with language.

Bateman's 'mask of sanity' is seemingly nowhere more securely in place than when he commits entire chapters to enthusing over his favorite popular music. The three privileged recipients of his admiration are now classic representatives of 1980s mainstream music: Genesis, Whitney Houston and Huey Lewis and the News. It is in the chapters devoted to them that Bateman's confidence is at its highest pitch; yet it is here that Ellis' satiric purpose with his voice is at its most barbed and subtle. To appreciate this satire, we must acknowledge the gulf Ellis designates and mourns bewteen the late-1970s/early-1980s phenomenon of punk music, and the corporate pop of the mid-1980s. The early scene describing the ridiculous punk-bohemian characters Stash and Vanden is our first clue to this layer of meaning in the novel, which then returns again and again to punk's death, like a tongue to a loose tooth (and remember, too, that their appearance in the first chapter is explicitly associated with an article in *Deception* entitled 'The Death of Downtown' — we will take this up later.)

In "Genesis", it is not so much punk as Peter Gabriel who is at the satiric kernel of the prose. After Gabriel's departure (and commitment to projects such as ending apartheid), the band's music "got more modern, the drum machine became more prevalent and the lyrics started getting less mystical and more specific . . . and complex, ambiguous studies of loss became, instead, smashing first-rate pop songs that I gratefully embraced" (p. 133). There can be no mistaking the irony in Bateman's uncritical embrace of a corporate aesthetic that abolishes intellectual content in the name of 'poppy and lighthearted' inanity. Ellis expects us to pay attention to the collapse of critical integrity here, a collapse fully articulated in the later chapter, "Huey Lewis and the News". Bateman's dismissal of this band's first LP on the basis that it is 'too punk' triggers our suspicions: ". . . they also carried with them some of the bleakness and nihilism of the (thankfully now forgotten) punk rock scene in Los Angeles at the time" (p. 353). Any reader of Ellis's first novel, *Less Than Zero* (where Costello figures as an icon, a talisman of integrity in a valley of shades), will note the information that it was Elvis Costello who discovered Lewis. But Bateman misidentifies the album on which Lewis played for Costello, and then goes on to declare a preference for Lewis over Costello on the basis of sales figures, dismissing Costello's intellectualism. Such distinctions are loaded with significance, and tilt the scales against Bateman's philistinism. Following albums from Huey Lewis leave behind the early 'bitterness' and nihilism and disport in good-humored tunefulness and 'relationship' songs. 'Frat guy sweetness' takes over from punk on *Sports*: a "clear, crisp sound and a new sheen of consummate professionalism" (p. 355). The track 'Hip to be Square' is especially admired as a "rollicking ode to conformity" (p. 357). Pop-musical taste is here being used as a means of gauging the degree to which Bateman's mind has in fact surrendered every critical impulse and gone over to the conformities of the entertainment industry. The final hope of *Less Than Zero* was contained in the 'harsh and bitter' imagery of the punk band X's song "Los Angeles", which resonated in Clay's mind like the promise of something else. In *American Psycho*, that promise has been smothered by corporate mediocrity.

ALIENATION AND REIFICATION

The next modality of Bateman's voice to repay critical attention is the voice of urban alienation, a clear vestige of the earlier period of modernism, most famously represented by T. S. Eliot. Unlike most of the novel, which takes place indoors, these scenes are typically exteriors, and tend towards more extreme literary effects. Chapters written in this mode are "A Glimpse of a Thursday Afternoon", "Shopping", and some of "Chase, Manhattan". Here, paragraphs stretch into endless, breathless concatenations of staccato clauses and phrases.

Loosening my suspenders, ignoring beggars, beggars ignoring me, sweat-drenched, delirious, I find myself in Tower Records and I compose myself, muttering over and over to no one, "I've gotta return my videotapes, I've gotta return my videotapes," and I buy two copies of my favorite compact disc, Bruce Willis, *The Return of Bruno*, and then I'm stuck in the revolving door for five full spins and I trip out onto the street, bumping into Charles Murphy from Kidder Peabody or it could be Bruce Barker from Morgan Stanley, *whoever*, and he says "Hey, Kinsley" and I belch into his face, my eyes rolling back into my head, greenish bile dripping in strings from my bared fangs . . . (pp. 150–51)

This clearly takes place on a different linguistic plane from the insipid everyday narration of other scenes. It too is characterized by what is called *parataxis*, or in other words the refusal of the prose to construct complex sentence formations, and the decision instead simply to run clauses and phrases alongside one another. However, here the units of meaning are that much shorter, more crowded together, leading to an effect of absolute desperation, acceleration and disintegration. Each clause, most of them beginning with 'and

then I', 'and I', offers a snapshot instantly replaced by the next one.
There is no continuity, no accord. Nor do the last quoted clauses
here, refering to the 'bile' and the 'fangs' really refer to anything
actually 'happening' at all. This is a frantically composed list of
clichés about urban paranoia, alleviated only by acts of consumption (two more copies of his favorite disc), and otherwise dominated
by panic and nausea. And Patrick's typical way of resolving such a
chapter is, of course, the redirection of all this panic and nausea
upon an ethnic minority. The chapter ends mid-sentence after some
extreme racist class hostility against a Jewish waitress: "Fuck yourself
you retarded cocksucking kike" (p. 152). Unlike modernist alienation, which drove its tensions inward, this postmodern kind ends
up in an explosion of pure class/ethnic hatred.

In "Shopping", after several impacted lists of the multitudinous
produce on display, Bateman seems to attain an insight into his
alienation: "Some kind of existential chasm opens before me while
I'm browsing in Bloomingdale's", he avers (p. 179). But lest we be
lured into thinking that he has made the connection between all
the commodities on offer and this 'existential chasm', he is quick to
assure us that "I decide this emptiness has, at least in part, some
connection with the way I treated Evelyn at Barcadia the other
night, though there is always the possibility it could just as easily
have something to do with the tracking device on my VCR ..."
(pp. 179–80). Anything and everything in Patrick's own life is actually a token of the 'chasm' in his being. The products themselves,
with their certain properties and price-tags, retain some relative
integrity. They emerge into view as more stable, more reliable and
more durable than Bateman's attitiude towards his girlfriend. And
there is a virutal infinity of them:

... paisley ties and crystal water pitchers, tumbler sets and office clocks that
measure temperature and humidity and barometric pressure, electric

calling card address books and margarita glasses, valet stands and sets of dessert plates . . . (p. 178)

Each can be approached and seduced with confidence and aplomb: "with my platinum American Express card I buy six tubes of shaving cream" (p. 179). Unlike a conversation with Evelyn, here is a victory over existence, a certainty. So that ultimately the 'chasm' in Bateman is bridged by the fact that "I'm wearing a cashmere topcoat, a double-breasted plaid wool and alpaca sport coat, pleated wool trousers, patterned silk tie, all by Valentino Couture, and leather lace-ups by Allen-Edmonds" (p. 180). Almost every chapter in the book contains this essential description of what Patrick is wearing. This is what we call *reification*, the transformation of relationships between human beings into relationships between things. Reification is both what is behind the urban alienation Patrick experiences, and his only method for curing it. The infinity of things through which he can identify himself opens up the 'existential chasm' in Bateman; he closes it briefly in the gesture of purchase.

"There are too many fucking videos", Bateman cries at one point, renting *Body Double* for the thirty-seventh time anyway. The writer Elizabeth Young has commented on this aspect of *American Psycho*, its manifest concern with the hollowing-out effects of consumerism and reification on human beings:

Within consumer capitalism we are offered a surfeit of commodities, an abundance of commodity choices, but this image of plenty is illusory. Our desires are mediated by ideas about roles and lifestyles which are themselves constructed as commodities and our 'choices' are propelled by these constructs. In a world in which the only relations are economic, we remain alienated from any 'authenticity' of choice or desire. Patrick has been so fragmented and divided by his insane consumerism that he cannot 'exist' as a person.[5]

This fragmentation is registered in the text through the stylistic devices of parataxis and list-making—the tendency of each sentence to break up into clauses which approximate a sales catalogue or advice column. In this way, Ellis designates the colonization of the psyche by prefabricated discourses, the reduction of thought to habitual reflexes of socialized language. The epigraph from Karl Marx at the head of this chapter suggests that it is only in the most developed and 'advanced' of societies that this leveling of behavior, thought and expression to a single, homogeneous level takes place, under the 'one feature common to all': namely, being a product or commodity.

Reification affects all of the discourses in which Bateman is written. Consider those passages where his sexuality is presented, mainly in the three chapters entitled "Girls". Here, where we might expect some semblance at least of spontaneity and the free expression of sexual affect, we have the hollowest pastiche of pornographic textuality. Sexuality is wholly inscribed here through the heavily stereotyped langauge of mass-marketed pornographic literature: "Sabrina is now face level at Christie's ass and cunt, both of which I'm fingering lightly. I motion for Sabrina to move her face in even closer until she can smell my fingers which I push into her mouth and which she sucks on hungrily. With my other hand I keep massaging Christie's tight, wet pussy, which hangs heavy, soaked below her spread, dilated asshole" (p. 173). The absence of all emotional content here is at one with the nature of the rhetoric, which works according to mathematical binaries: ones and twos, ups and downs, overs and unders. The voice itself, the origin of authority, disengages itself from the formalised action it instigates, such that at moments it is stranded in its own boredom: "Tired of balancing myself...", "My cock slides in almost too easily...". Nothing springs naturally from the situation. The tableaux which the voice imposes on the three bodies proceed from already-read porn literature and already-seen porn videos. The women are only there because they are being paid. If there is pleasure, it is a pleasure purely of reification: the transformation of intensely private human relations into things, tableaux, props, prices. And we are implicated here, as readers. As Ellis has said with regard to his use of pornography, "I'm interested in how pornography affects a reader. It's such a consumer item. It does what it's supposed to do.... Since it's such a consumer good and because the book is so full of consumer goods, why not throw in some porn amidst all the clothes and all that useless hipness?"[6]

Even when Patrick is with a lover, the transition from intimate contact into reification is rapid. "Wait," cries Courtenay, a few 'thrusts' into intercourse. *"Is it a receptacle tip?"* The condom must be scrutinized. No; it is a plain tip, unable to " 'catch the force *of the ejaculate!'* " Meanwhile, Patrick is concerned that "the goddamn *water-soluble spermicidal lubricant"* is not being used. Once everything is in order, they can get back to business. "Roughly I push my cock back into her and bring myself to an orgasm so weak as to be almost nonexistent" (pp. 103–105; stresses in original). Consumer goods intervene between human agents to the point that they displace anything resembling feeling; pleasure is knowing you're using the right lubricant. The obvious comedy is laced with the most despairing social vision.

THE VIOLENCE OF *AMERICAN PSYCHO*

The most disturbing thing about Bateman's sexuality, however, is not that it is reified by stereotyped language and paraphernalia, but that it segues into the excruciating violence of the book's most notorious passages. I want to insist that these factors are intimately related, however. Bateman's sexual/textual violence is a symptom of the waning of sexual feeling under the regime of commodities in which he functions. It is also, as I have already suggested, a symptom of the fact that there is no sexual relation possible in the text; that, in the strictest possible sense, men and women occupy distinct planes of being here, unable to connect or relate apart from moments of consumption (in restaurants, as sex-workers and clients, with the products of the contraception industry, or literally, as in "Tries to Cook and Eat Girl"). It is important to note, however, that sexual violence only appears in the book's second half, and that the first three narrated acts of violence are committed against men and dogs: the black homeless man Al and his dog Gizmo, the nameless 'old queer' and his Sharpei Richard, and a Chinese delivery boy. It is not until the culmination of the first episode with the prostitutes Christie and Sabrina, that Patrick first fully intimates the ferocity of his sexual appetite, notably in the future tense: "Tomorrow Sabrina will have a limp. Christie will probaly have a terrible black eye and deep scratches across her buttocks caused by the coat hanger" (p. 176). Even here, we are given nothing in the present, and everything could well be contained to the level of fantasy; we might read Patrick's malevolent bombast the way his companions read his fascination with serial killers — as so much empty blather.

Such a hypothesis is compromised by the incidents narrated at the end of a long chapter, "Lunch with Bethany"; Bethany being an old girlfriend of Patrick's whom he has met again coincidentally. These incidents — her beating with the nail gun, her being nailed to wooden boards, his Macing of her face, his biting off her fingers, stabbing her breasts, cutting out her tongue, etc. — are so confronting and disturbing partly because they have been so long in coming (this is two-thirds into the book), and partly because what had remained latent behind all the surface banality is here given such swift and explicit expression that we are simply unprepared for it. Two points must be made, however. First, Bethany is *not* part of the social world Bateman now inhabits; indeed, she is a throw-back to his past at Camden College, and so what 'happens' to her cannot be checked by anyone Patrick now knows. This is critical, and links her fate neatly to that of Al, the 'old queer' and the delivery boy, as well as the two prostitutes. Second, Bethany has been guilty on their date of two unforgivable acts of 'violence' against Patrick's monumental egotism: she confesses that her boyfriend is Robert Hall, the chef and co-owner of Dorsia, the restaurant at which Patrick has no success in booking tables; and she tells him, giggling, that his prize *objet-d'art*, his David Onica painting, is hung upside down on his living room wall. She has thus one-upped him socially as well as culturally, and Bateman's language is nowhere more pointedly in crisis: "Yes, my brain does explode and my stomach bursts open inwardly — a spastic, acidic, gastric reaction; stars and planets, whole galaxies of little white chef hats, race over the film of my vision" (p. 239). This reference to the 'film' of Patrick's vision is taken up again when he finally decides to kill Bethany: "As if in slow motion, like in a movie, she turns around" (p. 245).

So, however graphic the violence is in its detailed objectivity, we should pay close attention to the ways in which Ellis has asked us to qualify Bateman's report. Of course, at the level of textual reality, the violence 'happens'; we are obliged to read through sentences detailing appalling acts. But the question is: what status do these sentences have? Everything hinges on the possibility that the graphic description is in fact so much impotent discursive *revenge* upon assaults against Bateman's infantile egotism. And here we really must turn again to the unexpected fact that this first 'sexual' murder (although, it is worth noting that no sex takes place apart from a final and aborted attempt at fellatio with Bethany's tongue-less mouth) is actually the text's fourth attempted murder; and that, in no conceivable psychological profile of any serial killer or mass murderer — two distinct types — would these four crimes be attributable to any one man. As Elizabeth Young says, "Ellis has . . . created a most unusual creature, a serial sex-killer who is also, at the same time, prepared to kill absolutely anyone."[7] We must ask ourselves: *what* links the four assaults to date? The answer is complex, and yet surprisingly simple: the precise mixture of envy and hate which determines Patrick's class consciousness as a yuppie.

Al's mutilation in "Tuesday" is contextualized by Bateman's stroll downtown below Fourteenth Street, where 'black guys' offer crack, 'skinny faggots' whistle and laugh at Bateman, and another yuppie urinates in the street: these clichés of urban vision alert us to the fact that the perimeters of the run-down Lower East Side are alien and hostile to Bateman's Uptown yuppie psyche. "Get a goddamn job, Al", sneers the Soprani-clad Bateman, on learning that Al, like so many working class African-Americans in the age of Reagan, has been laid off. The fierce description of Al's mutilation is followed by another sneer: "There's a quarter. Go buy some *gum*, you crazy fucking *nigger*" (p. 132). The violence as such is really a narrative elaboration—what Eliot called an 'objective correlative'—of an entire system of race and class prejudice which underlies the encounter. And although there is a late chapter ("Bum on Fifth") in which we appear to be reacquainted with the now disabled Al and Gizmo after a year's interval, that chapter ends with assertions that "On *The Patty Winters Show* this morning a Cheerio sat in a very small chair and was interviewed for close to an hour"; and "I buy a Dove Bar, a coconut one, in which I find part of a bone" (p. 386). This (along with the fact that no uninsured homeless person could have survived Bateman's attack) calls into ultimate doubt the mutilation of Al on anything other than an allegorical and political level, as the expression of class hatred.

Similarly, the murder of the 'old queer' is doubly motivated by contempt and envy; homophobia on the one hand, and envy for the possession of the precious Sharpei (already declared) on the other. The murder, which needlessly utilizes both knife and gun, is concluded with another ludicrous and 'unreal' cinematic moment: ". . . and I'm running down Broadway, then up Broadway, then down again, screaming like a banshee, my coat open, flying out behind me like some kind of cape" (p. 166). The delivery boy whose throat Bateman improbably 'slits open' is perceived as a Japanese, and as Charles Murphy has just been prompting Patrick, the Japanese are buying up all of Manhattan, "the Empire State Building and Nell's. *Nell's*, can you believe it, Bateman?" (p. 180). (This is a persistent fear of yuppies in the novel; later, Harold Carnes will lecture Bateman: "Face it . . . the Japanese will own most of the country by the end of the '90s", p. 386.) In this regard, the boy's murder is an enactment of the racist fear and envy contained in that exasperation; with the stupidly comic denouement that Bateman of course can't tell a Japanese from a Chinese, and all the spilled 'beef chow mein' and 'moo shu pork' drives home the realization that he has accidentally killed "the wrong type of Asian" (p. 181). This is quite absurd, and its purpose is to feed backward into previous assaults, and forward into following ones, contaminating them all with the latent suspicion that what the text presents as violent acts, are in fact to be considered as the cinematically projected fantasization of a general class violence towards everything that is not white, male and upper-middle class.

This is a theory which meets its ultimate challenge, not in the abominable sequence in which Bateman lures a starving rat up a girl's vagina through a Habitrail tube (for here the girl is flatly nameless, a mere cipher whose nonexistence has surpassed even the made-up names of 'Tiffany' and 'Torri' in the previous "Girls" chapter), but in the chapter which most deliberately authenticates itself as the narration of a real murder: "Paul Owen". I have already insisted that the other murders happen to characters who have no reality in the social world Bateman inhabits, who can be construed

as imagined grounds upon which he constructs his class consciousness through the language of ultra-violence. Paul Owen, however,
is a well-known figure in the center of Bateman's universe; in fact
he *is* the center, the sun around which Bateman and his interchangeable companions circle in emulation and envy. In order to
lure Owen back to his apartment, Bateman has willingly exploited
the fact that Owen has no idea who he is, going along with his
misapprehension that Patrick is actually Marcus Halberstam. As
Halberstam, Bateman reserves a table in the unpopular Texarkana
for two, and he and Owen meet there on what is, for all intents and
purposes, a date (there is a possibility that Patrick is actually 'gay').
Bateman's purpose is to get to the bottom of the legendary 'Fisher
account' for which Owen enjoys exclusive responsibility. The Fisher
account is something like the Holy Grail of the investment-banking
world all these men inhabit: presumably worth billions, and carry-
ing with it arcane secrets and privileges, it is the secret of Patrick's
desire. Like a true member of the elite, Owen relates only banal
information about it, and "infuriatingly changes the topic back to
either tanning salons or brands of cigars or certain health clubs or
the best places to jog in Manhattan" (p. 216). Owen's tactics declare
a limit to Bateman's solipsistic omniscience, and by so doing insti-
gate the desire to kill. Bateman's envy of the Fisher account, and
his realization that he will never control it, prompt the text miraculously to transport both men back to Bateman's apartment in a
single clause—a literary jump-cut. Here, Bateman can happily cut
Owen to pieces with an axe.

Pay attention to the degree to which linguistic competence during the 'murder' outstrips Bateman's performance at Texarkana,
where he had been heard to utter "Is that Ivana Trump over there?
. . . Jeez, Patrick, I mean *Marcus*, what are you *thinking*? Why
would Ivana be at Texarkana?" (p. 215). This stylistic drivel fades in
light of the relative mastery of the later description: "Blood starts to

slowly pour out of the sides of his mouth shortly after the first chop, and when I pull the ax out—almost yanking Owen out of the chair by his head—and strike him again in the face, splitting it open, his arms flailing at nothing, blood sprays out in twin brownish geysers, staining my raincoat. This is accompanied by a horrible momentary hissing noise actually coming from the wounds in Paul's skull, places where bone and flesh no longer connect, and this is followed by a rude farting noise caused by a section of his brain, which due to pressure forces itself out, pink and glistening, through the wounds in his face" (p. 217). Here, as nowhere else, Bateman's voice is capable of complex sentence formation, clausal subordination, detailed analyses of material processes, descriptive verve, adjectival and adverbial precision, and bravura periods. It is a light year away from "I get on top of her and we have sex and lying beneath me she is only a shape, even with the halogen bulbs burning" (p. 213), in the immediately preceding chapter. Paul Owen has been transformed from a character into a thing from which to produce sentences that in turn anatomize him into parts. Bateman is not so much murdering him, as he is getting good syntactical mileage out of Owen's highly imaginative, attentive destruction. This is not the prose of someone hacking someone else to death in the heat of the present tense; it is the prose of someone lovingly contemplating the thought of hacking someone to death in the eternal slow-motion of pure solipsism.

The violence in the book should be understood as an act in language, the attainment of a certain kind of literary flair, which is elsewhere obviated by reification, repetition, and inanity. It is an act in language which is undergirded and informed by a profound race and class arrogance, homophobia, misogyny, and solipsistic vanity. But its effect is to launch these passages on to a different stylistic plane, which is really one of the major reasons that these passages leave such an impression. That is to say, the violence is not simply a matter of *content*; it is very much a matter of *form* and *style. Form,* because we have to wait so long for any signs of literary distinction (the text otherwise being an object lesson in 'bad' writing), that when they finally arrive we feed on them hungrily, even though they occur in scenes of abomination; and *style*, because it is here that the oppressive paratactic narrative voice finally 'lets rip' and tips over from weightless indistinction into driven, compulsive syntactical constructions.

In terms of the reliability of our narrator, the question is: what really happens to Paul Owen? All we can say with certainty is that he disappears—a private detective is put on the case by his girlfriend. (Owen is not the first character simply to vanish from the text. Earlier, Tim Price, the friend with whom Patrick rides to Evelyn's house in the first chapter, takes a stroll down the tunnel in Tunnel club, not to be seen again for a good year.) Patrick tells us that he has Paul Owen's keys (after putatively having dumped his body in a vat of acid), and manufactures a departure for Owen to London, including an answering-machine message to that effect (which sounds curiously like Owen's own voice). He then uses Owen's apartment to torture and butcher two prostitutes, Torri and Tiffany, in the most lavishly described detail, leaving their mangled and decomposing remains in the apartment, while fending off questions from the detective as to his relationship with Owen. However, the detective has already found an iron-clad alibi for Bateman which puts him in the company of his usual companions, including Marcus Halberstam, the man as whom he had posed with Owen on the night of the murder. The two key events, however, which finally round on the narrating voice and render its account of every violent act uselessly suspect, occur in the chapters "The Best City for Business" and "New Club".

"The Best City for Business" is a pivotal chapter in the novel; its function in the present context is to make Patrick Bateman's narration of his violent acts highly doubtful. Bateman has been fishing for news or rumour about the two sex workers he claims to have murdered in Owen's apartment, but "like in some movie no one has heard anything, has any idea of what I'm talking about" (p. 367). The 'movie' reference again is a key to the status of Bateman's violent activities. Returning to the 'scene of the crime' to sate his curiosity, he advances into the building, which 'looks different'. However, the keys he has do not fit the lobby door; nor will they fit the apartment door. A doorman shows him in, seemingly expecting him, directing him ahead to Mrs. Wolfe, a real estate agent. The elevator attendant with whom he rides up to the 14th floor is also a 'new addition' to the building. Upstairs, Owen's apartment is being shown. It is antiseptically clean, bedecked with dozens of bouquets, and the television plays low-volume commercials about stain removers: "but it doesn't make me forget what I did to Christie's breasts, to one of the girl's heads, the nose missing, both ears bitten off . . . the torrents of gore and blood that washed over the apartment, the stench of the dead. . . ." (p. 368). Of course, we think he doth protest too much. At this late stage of the game, the incommensurability between what Patrick 'remembers', and the "distressingly *real*-looking, heavily lipsticked mouth" of Mrs. Wolfe (a sly reference to Tom Wolfe's role in the text, as the literary 'Realist' who took on the same material with different aesthetic principles in *The Bonfire of the Vanities*), is all we readers need to connect the dots in this chapter (no rumor about deaths, different-looking building, unfitting keys, new attendant) and conclude that Bateman has never been here before. In confirmation of this, we might consider the descriptions of Owen's furniture in either chapter (Ellis has advised his readers to pay close attention to 'the language, the structure, the details'). In "Girls", Patrick notes only the following contents of Owen's 'ridiculous-looking condo': a black leather couch, a strip of faux-cowhide paneling, a futon, and an oak and teak armoire. Later, in "The Best City for Business", he tells us this: "New venetian blinds, the cowhide paneling is gone; however, the furniture, the mural, the glass coffee table, Thonet chairs, black leather couch, all seem intact. . . ." (p. 368). The tone of implacable certainty occludes the fact that Bateman has made only one 'hit': the black leather couch which, in 1989, was *de rigeur*. Bateman has simply not seen the place before. Or, that is at least one reading available to us, a lethal and important layer of meaning here — our narrator is not only unreliable, but worthless and thrown into a discursive tizzy when forced into recognition of this fact: "All frontiers, if there had ever been any, seem suddenly detachable and have been removed, a feeling that others are creating my fate will not leave me for the rest of the day. This . . . is . . . not . . . a . . . game . . ." (p. 370). So far from being able to create his own fate as story-teller, Bateman is at last obliged to realize his ineffectual passivity and hollowness as a protagonist-narrator.

The point is amplified in the "New Club" chapter a few pages later. Having confessed in the remarkable "Chase, Manhattan" section to "thirty, forty, a hundred murders" into Harold Carnes's answering machine (p. 352), Patrick here finally confronts Carnes and awaits his judgment. Inevitably, Carnes mistakes Bateman for "Davis", and approves of the joke he thinks Davis has made on Bateman by having him confess to so much violent crime. Not wholly however; the joke has one flaw, as he tells Bateman in an assumed English accent: " 'your joke *was* amusing. But come on, man, you had one fatal flaw: Bateman's such a bloody ass-kisser, such a brown-nosing goody-goody, that I couldn't fully appreciate it' " (p. 387). Here, in what for Patrick must be his greatest moment of exposure and shame, is what a first person narrator can never normally attain: a moment of objective self-knowledge, reached through the mistaken identity of a third person. Nothing could less fit our own 'knowledge' of Bateman by this stage, of whom we have come to think rather as one of the most evil characters in literary history. Yet Carnes's assessment carries on. In contrast Bateman's version of events, we learn that it was Evelyn who really dumped Patrick (an accusation Bateman does not in conversation deny). And Patrick could "barely *pick up* an escort girl", let alone "chop her up".

Finally, after Bateman insists on one definite fact, that he has killed Paul Owen and enjoyed it, Carnes tears even this vestige of his notoriety to shreds: " 'But that's simply not possible. . . . Because . . . I had . . . dinner . . . with Paul Owen . . . twice . . . in London . . . *just ten days ago.*' " To which Bateman can only feebly answer " 'No, you . . . didn't.' But it comes out a question, not a statement" (p. 388). Of course, there are ironies to Carnes's version of events, not least that he mistakes Bateman's identity, twice, and so may well have mistaken Owen's; but the lesson inheres in Patrick's absolute lack of fiber here, his virtual concession as narrator of everything Carnes has just said. His decision to include this conversation in the text, and not fight the resultant collapse of his entire narrative construction, is devastating. Bateman has, we may well conclude, done nothing but write, speak, construct himself in a variety of language games, none of which is any more 'real' than the others. Has he really not killed anybody at all? "Could be," says Ellis. "But I'd never commit myself on that. I think it important that fiction is left to the reader. That's the great thing about books."[8] All we can say for sure is that Patrick Bateman is, precisely, a fiction.

FICTION OR METAFICTION?

In fact, Bateman's fictionality is of the highest self-consciousness, and suggests an aggravated dance between him and Ellis himself, a shifting power relation between author and narrator, which is of the

highest order of interest theoretically; but, I feel, tends to diminish
the stylistic dynamics between the various language-zones outlined
above. That is to say, it is where Patrick comes into greatest self-
consciousness as a *non-self*, where the thematic interest of a lack of
individuality and a terrible one-dimensionality achieve most articulate expression, that the book violates its own stylistic law of 'inside-
ness' or immanance. The book is, however, most quotable here, at
its metafictional peaks:

Soon everything seemed dull: another sunrise, the lives of heroes, falling
in love, war, the discoveries people made about each other.... There
wasn't a clear, identifiable emotion within me, except for greed and, possibly, total disgust. I had all the characteristics of a human being—flesh,
blood, skin, hair—but my depersonalization was so intense, had gone so
deep, that the normal ability to feel compassion had been eradicated, the
victim of a slow, purposeful erasure. I was simply imitating reality, a rough
resemblance of a human being, with only a dim corner of my mind
functioning. Something horrible was happening and yet I couldn't figure
out why . . . (p. 282)

Here, everything that we really ought to have been deriving from
the rest of the book as attentive readers, comes into sharp and
unwonted focus. The very clarity of the phrases, the philosophical
nuance of the exposition, rubs against Bateman's otherwise imbal-
anced and disordered language games. Much later we read, ". . .
there is an idea of Patrick Bateman, some kind of abstraction, but
there is no real me, only an entity, something illusory, and though
I can hide my cold gaze and you can shake my hand and feel flesh
gripping yours and maybe you can even sense our lifestyles are
probably comparable: *I simply am not there*" (pp. 376–77). This
degree of metafictionality, this busy interference by the author with
his own creation, to show us that he knows how illusory all of his

effects are as fiction, tends nevertheless towards a kind of hectoring and bullying, an exasperation *avant la lettre* with all the likely complaints about the book as "an instruction manual in how to kill women" (see next chapter).

The philosophical streak of the book, its occasional tendency to formulate its own thematics in quotable statements, spills over from Bateman's concern with his own status as a character, and into more grandiose statements on yuppie morals and worldviews:

Sex is mathematics. Individuality no longer an issue. What does intelligence signify? Define reason. Desire — meaningless. Intellect is not a cure. Justice is dead. Fear, recrimination, innocence, sympathy, guilt, waste, failure, grief, were things, emotions, that no one really felt anymore. Reflection is useless, the world is senseless. Evil is its only permanence. God is not alive. Love cannot be trusted. Surface, surface, surface was all that anyone found meaning in . . . this was civilization as I saw it, colossal and jagged . . . (pp. 374–75)

Obviously these sentiments, exposed to merciless critique by Ellis himself, lie at the core of what *American Psycho* is protesting; but it is at least slightly discomfiting to have the words emerge from the fictional 'mind' of a character who is elsewhere so completely trapped by what they portend into reification, habit, repetition, pedantry and lurid fantasy. The dividing-line between fiction and metafiction is dangerously thin here, a layer of crisp ice which does not sufficiently bear the weight of repeated reading, nor, even, perhaps, a diligent first reading. What is more, Ellis cannot refrain from accentuating Bateman's fictionality at a more banal contextual level, which has eroded over time. As Elizabeth Young points out, "We know of his [Bateman's] *fictional* existence. He is the big brother of Sean Bateman in *The Rules of Attraction* and has already made an appearance in that book. He works at Pierce and Pierce which was Sherman McCoy's investment firm in *The Bonfire of the Vanities*. He knows people from other 'brat-pack' novels; Stash could be the person of the same name in [Tama Janowtiz's] *Slaves of New York*. Patrick tells of a chilling encounter with Alison Poole, heroine of Jay McInerney's *Story of My Life*. It seems as though Ellis is reinforcing the fact that Patrick's only existence is within fiction."[9]

Of course, Ellis is neither the first nor by any means the greatest exponent of metafiction in the American novel. Nabokov had played brilliant games with the reader on this borderline between narrator and author, in *Lolita* and *Pale Fire* above all. Perhaps the most outstanding of American authors to plough this furrow, how-ever, has been Thomas Pynchon; and it is enough for the reader to bear in mind the superlatively adept shifts in register which signal, say, Oedipa Maas's or Tyrone Slothrop's 'fictionality' in the elastic and expansive prose-style of a Pynchon text, to see how thin and unremarkable these moves are in Ellis's less capacious hands. Where Ellis is at his strongest is in marking the unbridgeable breaks between reified uses of language in Bateman's monologue. It is in these breaks that the 'depersonalization' and '*not-thereness*' of the contemporary human being can best be measured and assessed; not in self-conscious sophomoric reflections on that state of being. Bate-man, says Ellis, drawing our attention to the incommensurable here, is *literally* a "mixture of GQ and *Stereo Review* and *Fangoria* . . . and *Vanity Fair*."[10] Some of the best moments in the book are realized when these gulfs between styles, registers and planes are brought into the frame of the very same paragraph, jostling each other as starkly paratactic sentences, thereby indicating the absence of any coherent, mediating center of subjectivity:

If I married Evelyn would she make me buy her Lacroix gowns until we finalized our divorce? Have the South African colonial forces and the

Soviet-backed guerrillas found peace yet in Namibia? Or would the world be a safer, kinder place if Luis was hacked to bits? My world might, so why not? There really is no . . . *other hand.* (pp. 157–58)

The bastard's wearing the same damn Armani linen suit I've got on. How easy it would be to scare the living wits out of this fucking guy. Kimball is utterly unaware of how truly vacant I am. There is no evidence of animate life in this office, yet he still takes notes. By the time you finish reading this sentence, a Boeing jetliner will take off or land somewhere in the world. I would like a Pilsner Urquell. (p. 275)

This kind of style tends towards list-making, with the implication that no end or meaning will ever be reached. Random, meaningless, shallow, perverse, such entries speak much more effectively of Bateman's avowed fictionality than his metafictional soliloquys. In this sense, Bateman 'is' really no more than a zone of language in which irreconcilable soundbites and regurgitated bits of mediaspeak clash and overlap; his 'psychosis' is a forced polyphony of language-games illustrative of contemporary identity, an identity without substance or centre. An identity that is a fiction, though not one that we write ourselves. It is ceaselessly written for us, in us and on us.

THE POLITICS OF *AMERICAN PSYCHO*

What is not a fiction is the fundamental social reality that Bateman represents in the work, which it was Bret Easton Ellis' purpose to highlight and satirize in *American Psycho*. However 'illusory' Bateman's violence can be argued to be at a literary level, its point is extra-textual and political in the most basic sense; that is to say, we have to read *American Psycho*'s violent moments at three distinct levels. First, the bare fact is that, textually, they *happen*: they affect the reader and the course of the narration with real intensity. Second, at the level of some putative diegetic 'reality' outside the solipsistic chamber of Bateman's monologue, they probably *do not happen*. And third, at a higher, allegorical level, they once again *do happen*: as we shall be seeing, the new ruling class of Reagan's America was inflicting all kinds of violence on workers, homeless people, ethnic minorities and women, in effect much worse than the lurid and rococo violence of Bateman's discourse. The trick is to read these episodes on all three levels at once.

In the final pages of the novel, Tim Price has returned from his mysterious sojourn at the other end of the tunnel, and the television at Harry's is showing George Bush Sr.'s inauguration, and discussing Reagan's lies about the Iran-Contra affair. Price, evidently changed by his experiences elsewhere, is intrigued by the incongruity between Reagan's appearance and his actual conduct: " 'I don't believe it. He looks so . . . *normal*. He seems so . . . out of it. So . . . *un*dangerous.' To which McDermott replies, testily: 'He *is* totally harmless, you geek. *Was* totally harmless. Just like *you* are totally harmless. But he *did* do all that shit . . .' " (p. 397). This is as close as the novel gets to a genuine political discussion. Price wants to feel, perhaps does feel outrage that the gap between appearance and reality in politics is widening: "He represents himself as a harmless old codger. But inside . . ." Inside, like Bateman himself, Reagan is the 'psycho' of the novel's title, selling arms to Iran to back genocide in Nicaragua. No one else cares; everyone is silently complicit. Elsewhere in the work, Bateman has explicitly identified himself with this 'psychotic' clique. Always ready with the tritest liberal media cliché about current affairs—"I just want everyone to know that I'm pro-family and anti-drug" (p. 157); "Most importantly we have to promote general social concern and less materialism in young people" (p. 16)—Bateman attends a fundraiser for Dan Quayle (p. 327), a Young Republican party at

Trump Plaza (p. 336), and has a poster of Oliver North in his apartment (p. 339). He declares open sympathy for the Nazis at one point (p. 156), and to his adoring secretary Jean "I could even explain my pro-apartheid stance and have her find reasons why she too should share them and invest large sums of money in racist corporations . . ." (p. 263). Putting all of this together, Bateman is clearly meant to figure as a pin-up boy for the establishment Right, a composite, exaggerated portrait of the then new political entity, the Young Urban Professional Republican of the 1980s, whose egregious political impetus spelt ruin for the very 'underclass' over which we repeatedly see him trample on page after page.

No reader of the novel will forget the use of the musical *Les Misérables* as a satiric key to the class politics of Bateman and his gang. As an allegorical device, Boublil and Schonberg's musical adaptation of Victor Hugo's great nineteenth century novel of social complaint, nicely, if rather repetitiously, underscores the bourgeois transformation of a polarized urban political context into an opportunity to consume and enjoy the image of misery. Hugo's original 'pity' for the victims of urban capitalism, is displaced by the musical adaptation into an all-dancing, all-singing extravaganza open only to the middle and upper class, who are content to spend more on tickets than they will all year on charity. We do not see the musical itself, but only the various hand-bills and CD soundtracks, so many visual and aural synecdoches of a commercial exploitation of the very misery it helps perpetuate. As an accompaniment to his pornographic power over the two prostitutes, the disc of *Les Misérables* perfectly complements Bateman's appetite for other people's unhappiness.

In a typical moment, McDermott and Bateman have just exited the nightclub Nell's with two 'Eurotrash hardbodies', when McDermott spies a homeless Black woman and her six-year old child, begging for food.

McDermott's eyes are glazed over and he's waving a dollar bill in front of the woman's face and she starts sobbing, pathetically trying to grab at it, but of course, typically, he doesn't give it to her. Instead he ignites the bill with matches from Canal Bar and relights the half-smoked cigar clenched between his straight white teeth—probably caps, the jerk.

'How . . . gentrifying of you, McDermott', I say. (p. 210)

Bateman here utters the very word which—I want to say—describes not only McDermott's but his own and everyone else's contemptuous attitude to the urban poor, the homeless, racial and ethnic minorities, and the working class. It is an attitude which eradicates the claim each of these groups has to humanity, reducing them to voiceless caricatures and stereotypes which can be enjoyed as the reflex of one's own unquestionable power to ride roughshod over their hungry bodies.

Bateman does not only spurn the 'underclass'. After his murder of the Chinese delivery boy, Patrick drives to Chernoble in Alphabet City, at the very heart of the bohemian and Black Lower East Side. Suddenly surrounded, not by his usual retinue of Wall Street slummers, but by 'punk rockers' and 'blacks', and bombarded not by Belinda Carlisle, but by the ominous sound of rap music, Bateman is told by two girls: "Go back to Wall Street . . . Fucking yuppie".

"Hey," I say, grinding my teeth. "You may think I'm a really disgusting yuppie but I'm not *really*," I tell them, swallowing rapidly, wired out of my head.

Two black guys are sitting with them at the table. Both sport faded jeans, T-shirts and leather jackets. One has reflector sunglasses on, the other has a shaved head. I stick out my hand at a crooked angle, trying to mimic a rapper. "Hey," I say. "I'm fresh. The freshest, y'know . . . like, uh, def . . . the deffest." I take a sip of champagne. "You know . . . *def*."

To prove this I spot a black guy with dreadlocks and I walk up to him and exclaim "Rasta Man!" and hold out my hand, anticipating a high-five. But the nigger just stands there.

"I mean"—I cough—"*Mon*," and then, with less enthusiasm, "We be, uh, jamming. . . ." (p. 199)

This deeply offensive bit of failed ventiloquism exposes the limits of Bateman's 'charm' (think, too, of his unrepeatable 'haiku' for Bethany), but also clearly shows the limits to which what I want to call his gentrifying agenda will go in the interests of urban cannibalism. *Gentrification* is, in some senses, a colonial activity: as a bourgeois attempt to 'upgrade' neighborhoods "with an influx of generally *private* investment" (according to the Real Estate Board of New York, Inc.), it pushes beyond the frontier of 'otherness' to bring back cultural rewards and ultimately control the space economically. Here, Bateman tries to mimic a rapper and a Rastafarian in excruciating bad taste; but his power as consumer, and that power multiplied by the size of his class, will ultimately allow him, imperially, to claim Alphabet City as his own. His despicable clichés will dominate where now they are still only failed sorties against the Other.

In one of the more intolerable chapters, "Killing Child at Zoo", we find the following passage, which neatly condenses what I am calling Bateman's gentrifying world view (that is, his latent wish to convert all of Manhattan into a consumer playground unspoiled by 'Otherness'):

Unable to maintain a credible public persona, I find myself roaming the zoo in Central Park, restlessly. Drug dealers hang out along the perimeter by the gates and the smell of horse shit from passing carriages drifts over them into the zoo, and the tips of skyscrapers, apartment buildings on Fifth

Avenue, the Trump Plaza, the AT&T building, surround the park which surrounds the zoo and heightens its unnaturalness. A black custodian mopping the floor in the men's room asks me to flush the urinal after I use it. "Do it yourself, nigger," I tell him and when he makes a move toward me, the flash of a knifeblade causes him to back off. All the information booths seem closed. A blind man chews, feeds, on a pretzel. Two drunks, faggots, console each other on a bench. Nearby a mother breast-feeds her baby, which awakens something awful in me. (p. 297)

The rest of the human race is sorted into types or species—drug dealers, niggers, faggots, drunks, blind men and mothers—all of which are dismissed as soon as they are named. The critical point of this episode is that the human 'zoo' into which Bateman's gentrifying lens converts the Central Park Zoo, is ringed in by the comforting "tips of skyscrapers, apartment buildings on Fifth Avenue, the Trump Plaza, the AT&T building", which surround the park. This symbolic encroachment of large capital on the unnatural 'zoo' of New York's unmonied majority is the very guarantee of Bateman's gentrifying optic, the basis of his arrogance and contempt. What is the history, what are the preconditions, of this kind of worldview?

Robert Fitch's book, *The Assassination of New York* (1993), charts in some detail the protracted history of the assaults of big capital against the urban working class. His fundamental argument concerns the fact that, since the World War II, a colossal transformation has taken place in the composition and 'use' of the city. Three-quarters of a million manufacturing jobs have been wiped out, and the ratio of manufacturing to office work (especially what he aptly calls FIRE: finance, insurance and real estate) has switched from 2:1 before the War to 1:2 today. This momentous transformation has had the full backing of the city authorities, and in essence represents what many theorists have been calling the 'postmodernization' of the big world city. The 'post-industrial' hypothesis (we are no longer in an age of industrial production, but one of 'services') suggests that increasing land-value in major cities depends upon the removal of old industrial sectors, squeezing out the factories (i.e., displacing them to the Third World), and letting multinational corporations erect skyscraper after skyscraper to rake in rental fortunes on office space. As Fitch says, "There is a nearly 1000 percent spread between the rent received for factory space and the rent landlords get for class A office space. Simply by changing the land use, one's capital could increase in value many times."[11] All the urban poor, *les misérables*, in *American Psycho* are in effect victims of a ruthless history of evictions and factory closures, which hinges on speculations in land rent. Bateman, who represents one of the three pillars of this process (finance capital), crystallizes the implicit ideology of the entire event: savage indifference.

The other side of this 'assassination' is the ground-level aspect of gentrification. Neil Smith's urgent work, *The New Urban Frontier: Gentrification and the Revanchist City* (1996), analyses this global phenomenon in a comprehensive sweep, but seizes on the particular history of the Tomkins Square riots in 1988, in the middle of Alphabet City, as his most salient illustration. It is crucial to note that Bret Easton Ellis was writing his novel in the immediate aftermath of this remarkable urban event. Tomkins Square had by the late 1980s become a veritable outdoor home for hundreds of Manhattan's unemployed and homeless people; in cardboard houses, and surrounded by the drug trade, these folk eked out their living under the shadow of Mayor Koch's indignant and gentrifying glare. On August 6, 1988, Koch and the NYPD set a 1 a.m. curfew to clear the Park: "The City", says Smith, "was seeking to tame and domesticate the park to facilitate the already rampant gentrification on the Lower East Side. GENTRIFICATION IS CLASS WAR! read the largest banner" (p. 3). The chant that erupted during the violent confrontation between the homeless and the police was "Class war, class war, die yuppie scum!" And the *New York Times* concurred with its headline of August 10: "Class War Erupts along Avenue B". The rallying cry went up around the city, among its teeming homeless and unemployed population: "Tomkins Square everywhere!" Indeed, the clash was one of the most important flashpoints of the entire Reagan era, a contagious cry of rage against an administration which had cut federal funding to the major cities by $26 billion. Yet the results were inevitable: "Block by block," writes Smith, "building by building, the area [of the Lower East Side] was converted to a landscape of glamour and chic spiced with just a hint of danger." Let these bare facts stand as an explanation for those moments in *American Psycho* when Bateman confronts 'Kill All Yuppies' graffiti and is told to "fuck off yuppie scum". Blame for the 'death of Downtown' is lain squarely at his feet. When Bateman calls McDermott's abhorrent dollar-burning 'gentrifying', he situates such behavior within a city-wide context of class struggle.

Yet, if this history is undoubtedly a major precondition of the production of the novel, and carries over into the text's manifest contents, there remains a major analytic and interpretive stumbling block. How are we meant to derive social lessons such as this from a text written entirely in the blinkered monologue of a solipsistic member of the very class whose self-interest depends upon the repression of such history? Doubtless, we would do well to believe Bret Ellis when he instructs us to pay attention to 'the details', since it is really only in the moments isolated above that the latent gentrifying content of Bateman's class consciousness gleams through the chinks in his protective armor of reified 'sanity' (i.e., stereotyped language-games, clichés and props). Otherwise, the fact that we are presented not with the Dickensian, or indeed Wolfian narratorial objectivity of Realism, but the hollowed-out monologue of a socially myopic compulsive consumer, means that we are implicitly invited *not to see* what Bateman cannot see. The fact is that the literary non-self which Ellis constructs with masterful relish is the only horizon of visibility in the text; so that anything we see beyond its suffocating, airless amodality of voice is glimpsed through an 'unconscious' slip, or through the opaque fog of ideology in which it is written. The text is not a history lesson; it is a lesson in the eclipse of historicity in the ideology of the yuppie class — with the ironic codicil that it was precisely this class which, liberated from social constraints and Keynesian 'corporatism' by Reaganism, was making history in its own repugnant image.

The chapter, "Chase, Manhattan", finally lays bare the implicit horror of such a world. On a ludicrous killing spree, Bateman makes a breathless dash through a 'gentrified' Tribeca toward the relative security of the Financial District, where he works. Upon entering what he thinks is his building, Patrick is forced to admit that the Julian Schnabel painting by the elevators belongs not to his firm but to another: he is in the wrong place, *he has moved buildings*. Shooting the Black nightwatchman and janitor in existential free-fall, Bateman flees across the street to his new building, where he can finally relax after his panic-stricken adventure on the 'mean streets' of downtown. So, although it is the promise of security, freedom and comfort for the yuppie class, enabling it to move onward and upward to larger, better offices, speculation on land-value in Manhattan creates as well this uncanny confusion of place. Architectural style is homogenized, the various corporate skyscrapers form one huge 'kaleidoscopic blur'. The flip-side of the dream of gentrification is this purely abstract space of identity and indistinction, the architectural equivalent of Bateman's unmodulated voice. A world created in the image of yuppies will ultimately look like this, like every American, European, Australian and Asian financial district — identical rearing skyscrapers and a street level erased of character by their 'mass murderous' interests. Which is precisely the reason Bateman makes raids on Alphabet City: a purely equivalent space is uninhabitable.

Nowhere is the uncanniness of the machinations of the market in real estate better realized than in the chapter called "The Best City for Business". Let us for the moment grant that Bateman does indeed, at least allegorically, kill Paul Owen, and then use his apartment to torture and butcher two prostitutes; the full force of what takes place in this late chapter can only take effect if at some level we believe it might all be true. And here, in the person of Mrs. Wolfe, is the real estate agent herself. Miraculously, she has transformed a human abatoir into a tantalizing living space. She is a figure out of a Kafka nightmare, a pure functionary invested with ultimate uncanniness. Her merest word is enough to rattle Bateman to the core.

"You saw the ad in the *Times*?" she asks.

"No . . . I mean yes. Yes, I did. In the *Times*". I falter, gathering a pocket of strength, the smell from the roses thick, masking something revolting. "But . . . doesn't Paul Owen . . . still *own* this?" I ask, as forcibly as possible.

There's a long pause before she admits, "There was no ad in the *Times*".

We stare at each other endlessly. I'm convinced she senses I'm about to say something. I've seen this look on someone's face before. Was it in a club? A victim's expression? Had it appeared on a movie screen recently? Or had I seen it in the mirror? It takes what seems like an hour before I can speak again. "But that's . . . his"—I stop, my heart skips, resumes beating—"furniture." I drop my umbrella, then lean down quickly to retrieve it.

"I think you should go," she says.

"I think . . . I want to know what happened". I feel sick, my chest and back covered with sweat, drenched, it seems, instantaneously.

"Don't make any trouble," she says.

All frontiers, if there had ever been any, seem suddenly detachable and have been removed, a feeling that others are creating my fate will not leave me for the rest of the day. This ... is ... not ... a ... game, I want to shout, but I can't catch my breath though I don't think she can tell. I turn my face away. I need rest. I don't know what to say. Confused, I reach out for a moment to touch Mrs. Wolfe's arm, to steady myself, but I stop it in midair, move it to my chest instead, but I can't feel it, not even when I loosen my tie; it rests there, trembling, and I can't make it stop. I'm blushing, speechless.

"I suggest you go," she says.

We stand there in the hallway facing each other.

"Don't make any trouble," she says again, quietly.

I stand there for a few seconds longer before finally backing away, holding up my hands, a gesture of assurance.

"Don't come back," she says.

"I won't," I say. "Don't worry." (p. 370)

This uncanny encounter between two agents of 'FIRE' (finance, insurance, real estate) opens a hole in Bateman's universe. Why? Bateman (representing finance capital) is the figure of *monetary* abstraction, while Mrs. Wolfe (representing real estate) is the figure of *spatial* abstraction. Bateman's 'work' — though we actually see him doing nothing — consists in the transformation of real industries, real production, into abstract numbers on the stock exchange, which his clients may buy or sell. This symbolic *murder of the real* by the abstract in the interest of profit is echoed on the allegorical level of the two dead prostitutes, whom Bateman has also murdered — Bateman is, on either level, the *murderer*. The apartment, meanwhile, is being subjected to a secondary process of abstraction. Mrs. Wolfe's work consists of making empty space consumable, transforming it into a desirable commodity. She redeems the 'murdered real' by *humanizing* it: all the roses, the cleanliness, the construction of habitability. This is another abstraction, of course; the smell beneath the scent of the roses if that of rot and decay. But the incommensurability of this order of abstraction — packaging —

with Bateman's order of abstraction — speculation — is what forces the language of Bateman into such Kafkaesque unease. The murderer is unwelcome at the ritual of redemption, however complicit they both may be. "Don't come back."

So, finally, what links Bateman's erasure of selfhood in a culture of consumerism with the historical and political realities of gentrification, is fundamentally this: gentrification (or, real estate) is really nothing other than the extension of consumerism to urban space itself. What happens to Paul Owen's apartment is what happens to the whole of downtown. The entire city, after having been 'murdered' (Fitch's word is 'assassinated') by finance capital, will gradually change into a gigantic Bloomingdales, where such commodities as 'Thai food', 'Black music' and 'bohemian chic' can finally be consumed as safely as a Tiffany watch, without the threat of real difference and politics. Bateman, the ideal consumer, his mental substance composed entirely of messages emanating from commodities, augurs this dismal realization. His 'mind' and the commercialized city of which it is a symptom — *the best city for business* — form a single Möbius strip, on which is imprinted a looped warning: ABANDON ALL HOPE YE WHO ENTER HERE. THIS IS NOT AN EXIT.

3

The Novel's Reception

Perhaps more than any other American work of the last twenty years, *American Psycho* can legitimately be labelled a scandalous novel, in the mould of *Lady Chatterly's Lover*, *Ulysses*, *Lolita* and *The Satanic Verses*. Like these great works, although perhaps without their literary genius, this book touched a nerve in the English-speaking countries where it was published, creating an 'event' which has not yet altogether passed. In some places, such as Australia, this 'event' is incarnate still in the cellophane wrapping and 'Restricted' sticker in which the book is packaged on the top shelf, for reasons of national censorship. The whole event has to do with the graphic sequences of sexual violence discussed in the previous chapter, and the scandal of these passages had erupted even before publication — and, taken out of context and splashed over the national media, that is no wonder.

Having spent three years on the manuscript, Ellis was certainly aware of the offensive nature of the book's violent sections, but believed that, when taken in the full context of the satiric and stylistic concerns of the novel as a whole, they would be properly understood. His agent, Amanda Urban, and his editor, Robert Asahina, had both assured him that the manuscript, while obviously containing disturbing material, was itself a relatively coherent and aesthetically interesting work. His publishers, Simon & Schuster, who had enjoyed the success of *Less Than Zero*, and expected a commercial come-back from *The Rules of Attraction* with this novel, had committed themselves to publishing *American Psycho* in December of 1990, thereby giving it the perfect release date as the ultimate piece of 'end-of-the-eighties' fiction. However, as the staff at the publishing house began circulating some of the more infamous passages among themselves, 'feelings of revulsion' were inevitably triggered. Imagine what would it have been like, as a young female staffer, to discover this on your desk one morning:

I'm trying to ease one of the hollow plastic tubes from the dismantled Habitrail system up her vagina, forcing the vaginal lips around one end of it, and even with most of it greased with olive oil, it's not fitting in properly. . . . I finally have to resort to pouring acid around the outside of the pussy so that the flesh can give way to the greased end of the Habitrail and soon enough it slides it, easily. "I hope this hurts you," I say.
. . . The rat doesn't need any prodding and the bent coat hanger I was going to use remains untouched by my side and with the girl still conscious, the thing moves effortlessly on newfound energy, racing up the tube until half of its body disappears, and then after a minute—its rat body shaking while it feeds—all of it vanishes, except for the tail, and I yank the Habitrail tube out of the girl, trapping the rodent. Soon even the tail disappears. The noises the girl is making are, for the most part, incomprehensible. (pp. 328–29)

This may be one of the more nauseating and despicable images in literature since de Sade, and seems out of context merely to indulge the worst kind of misogynistic voyeurism and disgust for the female body. Inevitably, this passage and some others were quickly leaked to the press, to *Spy* and *Time* magazines, so that the disgust of the in-house staff could be shared by millions.

Within a month of the final publication date, with thousands of copies of the book waiting in the wings, the unthinkable happened. Simon & Schuster dropped the book in a breach of contract, sacrificing their $300,000 advance to prevent an inevitable avalanche of media protest. The impact on Ellis was extreme; he says, "It was really shocking. This was the last thing in the world I thought would've happened. I thought maybe they would publish the book and maybe people would be upset by it, I guess, but I never thought they would *not* publish the book . . . , or the book would cause this kind of fury. I just didn't think this was going to happen. I didn't think there was enough in the book to make it that shocking."[12] Relatively, he is right: perhaps five percent of the book consists of (narratorially dubious) violent episodes. That these episodes are memorable and extreme is incontestable, but most of *American Psycho* is a mind-numbing exercise in satirized banality, whose latent violence it was the function of the violent scenes to allegorize.

Although Vintage, a subsidiary of Random House, laid out another generous advance and took the cancelled book on — doubtless with an eye to the media interest as a guarantee of sales — the damage to the novel's reputation was severe. Most of the media firestorm erupted before anyone had seen the manuscript or read a word besides the leaked passages. Of course, there were liberal voices who condemned the Simon & Schuster decision as an act of lamentable, un-American censorship; especially as it appeared that the decision to axe the novel depended on the moral distaste of Martin Davis, the chairman of Paramount Communications, Simon & Schuster's corporate parent. The president of the National Union of Writers, Jonathan Tasini, said: "When a corporate executive like Richard Snyder or Martin Davis can censor an author based on their tastes or morality, society is taking one more giant leap toward corporate control of the world."[13] The irony was lost on nobody that Martin Davis's company had produced the *Friday the 13th* slasher movies. However, the publishing house denied that Davis had had any role in the decision.

Most of the voices in the press were denunciatory. Lorrie Moore, the acclaimed novelist and story writer, was rightly careful to distinguish what she called a 'botched rejection' from an act of censorship (which can only descend from government), but then went on to approve of any publisher's freedom not to publish a book 'for reasons of taste', and to suppose (not having read the book, but being given ample space to write about it anyway) that Bret Ellis was a mere adolescent pornographer. Going much further, and based on as much familiarity with the text, the Los Angeles chapter of the National Organization for Women (NOW) called for a boycott of *American Psycho*. Its grounds were that, fundamentally, the book was nothing more than "a how-to novel on the torture and dismemberment of women." Tammy Bruce, the president of the L.A. chapter, was not calling on Random House not to publish; she was calling on members and the public at large to "exercise their right of free expression by refusing to buy the novel so the publisher 'will learn violence against women in any form is no longer socially acceptable.' "[14]

The most remarkable intervention from the opposition came, however, from some knowledge of the text. Roger Rosenblatt, columnist for *Life* magazine and essayist for the *MacNeill/Lehrer Newshour* (a favourite of Tim Price and the other yuppies in the novel), offered a piece to the *New York Times* sensationally entitled "Snuff This Book! Will Bret Easton Ellis Get Away With Murder?"[15] Rosenblatt's journalistic epithets were splashed all over the piece: 'moronic', 'sadistic', 'loathsome', 'pointless', 'themeless', 'everythingless', 'lame and unhealthy', 'worthless', 'junk'. He condemned Ellis's efforts as sub-literary and offensive to women, and applauded the good taste of Simon & Schuster. His final rallying cry to the literate population of America chimed perfectly with the NOW boycott: 'don't buy it.' "That nonact would give a nice ending to our tale. It would say that we are disgusted with the gratuitous degradation of human life, of women in particular. It would show that we can tell real books from the fakes. It would give the rasp-berry to the culture hustlers who, to their shame, will not say no to obvious rot. Standards, anyone?"

But surely the only standards being violated here are literary critical ones, since Mr. Rosenblatt would appear to have forgotten the simple distinction between the "gratuitous degradation of hu-man life" and an act of literature which wants to denounce that very degradation. In Mr. Rosenblatt's estimation, the act of not buying *American Psycho* would amount to a blow for women against their degradation at the hands of men such as Ellis, and at the same time reinstate a clear sense of good literary taste. Yet the degradation of women surely occurs first and foremost at the frontline of the fashion industry and the patriarchal logic of a nation which refuses women equal pay and full rights over their own bodies; and 'good literary taste' not only will have nothing to say about these things, but may even positively buttress them and ensure their survival. Bateman's misogyny is a relfex, a symptom, of the fact that his 'taste' in women is based on an absolute divorce between him and 'them' at every level: culturally, psychologically, emotionally, intellectually, professionally, etc. And this divorce, this absolute abyss over which women can only be perceived as consumable objects, is culturally prescribed and determined. It is the very culture whose 'standards' Mr. Rosenblatt wants to see preserved that is making sure 'Patrick Bateman' can exist as a potential reality.

Ellis's first line of defence fell to that old literary pugilist and defender of free speech, Norman Mailer, who wrote in *Vanity Fair* that the very intolerability of Ellis's material, not its artistry, was what guaranteed its worth and interest. Mailer understood Ellis's disgust with the moral and political nightmare of the 1980s in America, and applauded his animus; but this general sympathy aside, Mailer still seemed critically at sea, unable to come to grips with the formal subtleties and aesthetics of the work itself. "Since we are going to have a monstrous book with a monstrous thesis," he wrote, "the author must rise to the occasion by having a murderer with enough inner life for us to apprehend him."[16] Nothing could fly so completely in the face of what Ellis had actually achieved; and it is a testament to his formal radicalism, his refusal to fashion forth anything resembling a coherent and believable central character with whom one might ultimately sympathize, that most of the critical complaints and defences alike fell foul of the habit of comparison. Both Mailer and Rosenblatt cite Dostoevsky as the inevitable point of contrast, since it was Dostoevsky who had first delivered a fictional murderer with sufficient psychological depth and complexity to have attained our genuine 'apprehension'. And of course, Ellis courts this comparison with his first epigraph, from *Notes from the Underground*, which explicitly associates his novel with Dostoevsky's. But critical comparisons such as this are almost always a sign of intellectual laziness. Rather than rest secure in a literary example some century old, surely the task is to come to terms with the formal law of the text at hand, and determine *why* Ellis should have created a psychological portrait with no depth. Mailer failed this task comprehensively.

In Britain, the terms of debate were no sharper. Fay Weldon attempted a rather insultingly illiterate defence of the novel in the pages of *The Guardian*. She saw the novel as a mirror held up unflinchingly to a world which is despicable and despises itself without acknowledging the fact; it is not the novel that is especially misogynistic, but the world it offers to represent. Her language, though, is banal and clunky: "This man Bret Easton Ellis is a very, very good writer. He gets us to a T. And we can't stand it. It's our problem, not his. *American Psycho* is a beautifully controlled, careful, important novel which revolves about its own nasty bits. Brilliant." And her final advice is at one with Rosenblatt's and Tammy Bruce's: "Look, I don't want you to actually read BEE's book. I did it for you."[17] Once again, asking the reader not to read the book is a way of avoiding the moment of trauma, of confrontation. John Walsh wrote some similar defensive things in *The Sunday Times*; but by and large the reaction was sub-intellectual, and revolved around the speculation that Ellis was evidently a warped and deranged individual, bleating his masturbatory fantasies onto the page for his own self-aggrandisement.

Ellis's own reaction was understandably mortified. How is it that his carefully constructed novel could so egregiously have been misread, misunderstood and villified as the very target it sought to satirise? How could the deliberate literary symptom be mistaken for the general social and cultural disease? The stupidity and bad faith of the notion of 'good taste' is what particularly galled the young writer, since if fiction is not to probe and lance the boils of contemporary society, then literature itself will amount to nothing but a sop to the status quo. Literature today, if it is serious, tends toward the extreme only because the object it is tracking — our very way of life — is also extreme: violent, crude, slick, murderous and deeply unjust. Any work of fiction that pretends to offer the consolations of 'good taste' today is little better than a band-aid on an internal hemorrhage. "Buy Alice Walker if it makes you feel better. Buy Amy Tan. I don't care what you read . . . !"[18] Ellis's exasperated cry still resonates.

4

The Novel's Adaptation

American Psycho was adapted into a film released in 2000. Directed and co-scripted by Canadian Mary Harron (the other co-scriptwriter was Guinevere Turner) for Lion's Gate Films (Universal), starring Christian Bale, Willem Dafoe and Chloe Sevigny, in its first year it grossed more than $15 million, for a production cost of only $8 million. This is not the film it might have been, however. Initially, the rights were optioned in 1991 as a David Cronenberg project starring Brad Pitt, which Ellis himself had scripted. During the 1990s, Cronenberg, who has made a career out of features dedicated to the perverse and the unpalatable, adapted two other classics of American alternative literature, William Burroughs' *Naked Lunch* (1991) and J. G. Ballard's *Crash* (1996), so Ellis's novel was an obvious attraction. However, it soon appeared that his ideas for the adaptation were unintelligible even to Ellis himself; as he described it, "David said, 'I want a screenplay that has no violence, so sex, no restaurant scenes, no club scenes, and I want it to be 60 pages long because it takes me two minutes to shoot a page.' I didn't know what he was talking about."[19]

When the project was offered to Mary Harron, who had made an impression with her film of the life and ideas of Valerie Solanas, *I Shot Andy Warhol* (1996), she quickly signed up Christian Bale as her ideal screen Patrick Bateman. The production executives at Lion's Gate, however, had the bright idea of dangling the project and a $20 million cheque before Leonardo DiCaprio, whose success in *Titanic* and global status as teen heartthrob would guarantee massive returns on their investments. At this point, asking if the executives were "on crack", Harron preferred to walk from the project than to compromise its integrity with a star who could not possibly capture the vicious emptiness of Bateman. Director Oliver Stone then looked poised to step in and make another ham-fisted, sledgehammer satire in the mould of *Natural Born Killers*, until DiCaprio (under the advice of his concerned agents and minders) accepted instead another $20 million fee to appear in *The Beach*. At which point, Harron and Bale returned to their previous roles.

The film as it now stands is a curiously satisfying and controlled social satire, which manages to retain much of the corrosive wit of the novel without indulging in the obvious temptations to screen violence. We must bear in mind the fact that, for the novel's Patrick Bateman, there is no act of violence that has not been mediated through the screen, whether large or small, and that for the most part the logic of his perceptions and actions in the violent sequences is explictly presented in terms of cuts, zooms and pans, and with all the creaking voyeurism of the 'video-nasties' he compulsively hires (there is even a possibility that Ellis himself is a real cultural conservative in this, and wants in part to blame the culture of screen violence for what Bateman actually says he is doing). So the challenge for Mary Harron was to arrive at a compromise between filtering the violence out altogether (making it too clear that Patrick does nothing), and graphically rendering the worst excesses of the novel's most infamous passages, reduplicating Patrick's lurid consciousness (which would militate against her feminist politics).

Her solution is intriguing. In only three scenes—the mutilation of Al (Reg E. Cathey), the murder of Paul Allen (not Owen in the film; played by Jared Leto), and the film's "Chase, Manhattan"—do we see Patrick doing what the book tells us he does. Al is stabbed, his dog stamped on, Paul Allen hacked to death with an axe, and various policemen and nightwatchmen are shot. On the other hand, the more notorious scenes involving the torture and murder of his women victims are, in contrast to the novel's forthright explicitness, highly elliptical and suggestive, and devaluate Patrick's authority over the proceedings. The long scene with 'Christie' (Cara Seymour) and 'Sabrina' (Krista Sutton) accentuates the women's discomfort and embarrassment; the camera significantly dwells on them during Bateman's excruciating monologue on Genesis and Phil Collins. As he barks instructions at them in the pauses between accolades for the music ("Get on your knees so Sabrina can see your asshole", "Sabrina, don't just stare at it—eat it"), the camera continues to register the women's acute embarrassment, while Bateman wanders in and out of the frame. And in the most powerful and significant addition to the scene, Harron has erected huge mirrors alongside the bed, into which Bateman stares as he fucks both women—at his own reflection while he pumps his biceps and hardens his abdominals. The point is obvious: Patrick can only desire his own self-image. When he finally gets out of bed to fetch his torture equipment, Harron inserts a jump-cut to the moment when both women, bruised and bleeding, take his money and leave the apartment. This kind of cinematic ellipsis is more effective from a feminist perspective than any representation of the violence itself, since it sacrifices all possibility of being read voyeuristically. We are confronted with the consequences, and not the perhaps titilating representation of misogynist violence.

Similarly, in the later scene in Paul Allen's apartement, when he has managed to lure 'Christie' back with an enormous amount of money to a session with his acquaintance Elizabeth (co-screenwriter Guinevere Turner), the camera assumes an unusual identification with 'Christie', whose face becomes virtually the fulcrum of the scene. On the one hand, this raises the stakes of the suspense, since an identification with the victim has been the essence of all great voyeuristic screen suspense (think only of *Psycho* and *Halloween*); on the other, it undoubtedly turns the tables on the narrative solipsism of Bateman himself, and inserts a kind of moral gaze which the sequence in the book decidedly lacks. Indeed, this kind of camera identification has already begun in the temptation scene in the alley, when 'Christie' initially refuses to have anything to do with the psychopath who abused her so badly last time that she "might need surgery". Here, in a very effective use of montage, the camera perspective alternates between Patrick's crouched point of view from inside the limo, of 'Christie's' scared and mistrustful face, and a hesitant, hand-held outside view which takes in the limo and 'Christie's' nervous body as she weighs up the possibility of violence against the cash being dangled in front of her. This differs from the novel, which simply presents everything from Patrick's point of view. We are asked here to glimpse Patrick's monstrosity from the outside, and to empathize with a woman who feels obliged to risk torture for a few hundred dollars.

The violence of the subsequent scene is reduced to a shot of blood soaking through the sheets as Patrick presumably bites Elizabeth, and her terrible shrieking, while 'Christie' makes a classic suspense-film dash through the apartment to find the door. On the way she discovers female cadavers in garment bags hanging in the cupboard, and another blood-soaked body on the bathroom floor, where Bateman catches up with her and tries to bite her leg. She lashes out and kicks him in the face (unlike the book, where nobody assaults Bateman) and escapes out of the apartment to the stairwell (again unlike the book, where she is tied to the futon and has her breasts electrocuted). The film permits her a few moments of hope, as she circles down the various flights of stairs to the bottom, while Bateman, naked, blood-spattered and gibbering, wields a running chainsaw on the top landing (a clear reference to Tobe Hooper's *The Texas Chainsaw Massacre*, which he has watched earlier while exercising). In a poetic moment, he drops the chainsaw at exactly the right moment, and watches as it falls to impale and tear through 'Christie' just as she is closest to actual escape. It is the most objectively unbelievable moment in the film, and is followed, in another jump-cut, by a shot of Bateman sketching a picture of a chainsaw ripping through a naked woman on a tablecloth in a restaurant where he is breaking up with Evelyn (Reese Witherspoon) — leaving us to ask: was it merely fantasy?

And that is it for violence against women in the film. There is no Bethany, no rat, no Torri or Tiffany, and although there is a blonde model that Patrick picks up at a bar, and we do see her head in his fridge in the next scene, we are shown nothing of what happens to her. Everything else is left to speculation and our own imagination, which has the effect both of making the sexual violence less of an obvious 'issue' in the narrative (less of a politically disabling distraction), and of creating the right air of doubt about it that the book can only produce through narrative crises instigated by third persons. Not that the film dispenses with these either, and both the real estate agent Mrs. Woolf (Patricia Gage) and Patrick's lawyer Harold Carnes (Stephen Bogaert) play the same crushing roles they play in the novel (while the detective, played eerily well by Willem Dafoe, also sticks his spanner in the narrative works). Harron shoots both of these menacing others in the same mask-like, frozen close-ups with which Stanley Kubrick had framed his actors in *The Shining* to destabilize Jack Torrance's (Jack Nicholson's) sanity and authority.

Nor does the film stop here in undermining the credibility of Bateman's violence towards women. The final scene at Harry's, where Carnes destroys Patrick's claims to homicidal mania, is inter-cut with a scene (impossible in the terms of the book's first person narration) of Patrick's secretary Jean (Chloe Sevigny) leafing through his diary alone in his office, where she discovers an escalat-ing number of poisonous doodles and designs devoted to the dese-cration of women's bodies, much like the various murders he claims to have committed. This scene clearly establishes the overriding possibility that Bateman's violence has all along been confined to the level of daydream and fantasy, and moreover scotches the pos-sibility left open in the novel that he and Jean will one day find a clichéd domestic life together. After such knowledge, what forgive-ness?

The great challenge in adapting *American Psycho*, however, was probably less in the violent contents, than in the fact that, as I argued in Chapter 2, Patrick Bateman is really little more than a jumbled array of language games—a verbal collage of disparate voices plucked from the magazines, instruction manuals and FBI files which served as Ellis's sources. *American Psycho* is, in that sense, a highly literary work, and lacks the requisite narrative drive to compensate for this discursivity when it comes to classic screen adaptation. Harron stays true to the absence of narrative—although she does significantly heighten the one true moment of suspense for Bateman (the interrogation by the detective) by drawing it out over three separate scenes instead of one—but is still necessarily barred from representing the essential literariness and 'fictionality' of Bateman on the screen due to his stable physical presence in the eroticised, almost fetishized body of Christian Bale.

There is a perrenial problem in adaptation of how to film a first-person narrative, and Harron's recourse to voice-overs which allow us into Bateman's head is a useful but insufficient device to represent the actual decentering and absence of Bateman as a subject in the novel's terms. The chiseled face and magnificent physique of Christian Bale constitute a sculptural corrective, a virtual icon standing against the insubstantiality and non-self of Bateman the 'character'; which is why, apart from a few early indulgences in describing his *levée*, Bale's voice-overs are generally confined to those textual moments discussed in Chapter 2 where Bateman achieves some unlikely philosophical insight to his own non-being. There is a striking moment in the opening segment where Bateman is peeling off his herbal face-mask while looking in the mirror, and we hear on the soundtrack the monologue from late in the book: ". . . there is an idea of Patrick Bateman, some kind of abstraction, but there is no real me, only an entity, something illusory, and though I can hide my cold gaze and you can shake my hand and feel flesh gripping yours and maybe you can even sense our lifestyles are probably comparable: *I simply am not there.*" While in the novel this can be criticized for an undue amount of self-consciousness, in the film it functions as a necessary shattering of the apparent plenitude of Christian Bale's perfect body as a refuge for our eyes. This, along with the increasing amounts of sweat, hysteria and panic imprinted on his face, is the film's principal means for denoting an absence within a luminous presence.

More generally, the coldness and affectlessness of Ellis's prose is interestingly registered in the film through a very muted colour scheme (revolving around a minimalist white, grey and red palette); a deadened and stylized, well-nigh Kubrickian dialogue delivery style; elegant frame compositions untroubled by agitated camera movements; and a score (by ex-Velvet Underground member John Cale) which utilizes a minimal string and piano orchestration in repetitious phrases that drain the frame of warmth and security without resorting to slasher-flick menace, dissonance or distortion. Thus an atmosphere of undoubted 'cool' and style is preserved, against which the violence — as in the book — appears as a tasteless, even comic shock (Bale's hammy monologue and body movements during the Paul Allen murder are very amusing). Harron wisely preserves all of the major comic moments (the business card show-down is especially good), while managing to derive an extra layer of satiric humor from the visual datedness of all the products and styles which in the book are merely mentioned verbally. The look of an early mobile phone (enormous and ugly), a slicked-back 1980s haircut, or a restaurant's pastel color scheme must all strike a con-temporary audience with the full force of the *passé* and the faintly ridiculous. In all these ways, Harron has done a commendable job of adapting what on first consideration may be thought of as an unfilmable novel; unfilmable as much for the tedious lack of nar-rative, and the sheer literariness of its major effects, as for the repulsive species of violence in its more infamous scenes. Con-firmed rumors that a sequel is being made which treats of a female 'escapee' from Bateman's violence merely underlines the fact, how-ever, that despite all Harron's and Ellis's efforts to problematize Bateman's account, viewers and readers alike may still take every-thing represented in the film and the novel with naïve literalness. The problem is if anything greater in the film version, since visual representation, however qualified, always forcibly suggests itself as 'realistic'. The novel's elaborate language games and intricacy of detail make it a more ambivalent and ultimately successful achieve-ment.

5

Further Reading and Discussion Questions

Is the violence in the novel misogynistic?

Although Bateman is a 'democratic' killer, and murders as many men as he does women (as well as a few animals), the sheer excess of his descriptions of the sexual torture, rape, dismemberment, desecration and abjection of women tilts the balance of the reading experience towards a disproportionate engagement with misogynistic violence. The question is: is this misogyny Ellis's or is it Bateman's? How is it possible to insert a barrier, of judgement and condemnation, between author and protagonist here? Is it enough for Ellis to say that it is 'obvious' that he doesn't himself feel this way towards women? Would the book have been improved by the excision of many of these scenes? Is it more important that we confront such abominations (since most of the details are taken from real cases) than that we turn away from them and pretend they do not happen? What is the function of literature: truth or the sanitation of reality?

Why is so much of the novel devoted to lists of commodities?

Many complaints about the novel concentrate on the sheer bore-dom of seemingly endless lists of products on the marketplace: stereo equipment, grooming products, accessories, chic food, de-signer clothes, etc. These passages are evidently not designed to please. So why are they there? Does Ellis produce a shock by confronting us, in a literary text, with what we confront daily any-way? Isn't an enormous amount of our time consumed by milling through thousands of products, and making spurious, empty choices based on taste or whim? Doesn't the monotony of the lists feed out into the rest of the book stylistically, so that at some limit everything in the book is just another list, even the torture scenes, and espe-cially the appearance of characters?

> "Then, almost by rote, as if I've been programmed, I reach for *Body Double*—a movie I have rented thirty-seven times—and walk up to the counter . . ."

Is there any free will in American Psycho*?*

Of course, every character is 'programmed' by his or her author, but few characters seem to have their actions so utterly prescribed as Patrick Bateman. Who is really dictating his actions? Is it the author, or is it not the market itself, prompting Patrick at every turn to buy this, rent that, order this, consume that? Isn't the desire to purchase, whether a diamond ring or a pizza, something emanating less from ourselves than from the ring or the pizza? If Bateman feels this way, isn't his response symptomatic of an entire culture of consumerism? Aren't we all compulsive shoppers? And why?

Is Patrick Bateman gay?

Although a Gay Pride parade down Fifth nauseates Patrick, and he is often to be found uttering homophobic epithets, there is a consistent hinting that he may himself be gay. His relationship with Luis Carruthers in particular, one of the novel's funnier storylines, is loaded with ambiguities. Luis reads Patrick's attempted strangulation in the Yale Cub toilets as a pass, and given how effective Bateman 'normally' is as a killer, he may have a point. A homoerotic graffito over the urinal seems to contain "an answer, a truth." Bateman is utterly paralyzed by Carruthers' turn, and cannot even say anything insulting.

Later, in 'Confronted by Faggot' Bateman is fully confronted with his possibly latent homosexuality (pp. 293–4); he has to say he doesn't find Carruthers "sexually attractive", but *not* that he is not gay. And it is among rows and rows of ties that Patrick has this confrontation with Luis—phallic symbols in serried ranks, which cannot ward off the incipient dissolution of Bateman's assumed sexual persona. How gay is Patrick?

> "I had to stop at Tower Records on the Upper West Side and buy ninety dollars worth of rap CDs but, as expected, I'm at a loss: niggerish voices uttering ugly words like *digit, pudding, chunk*."

What is at stake in Bateman's extreme racism?

The 'haiku' that Bateman composes for Bethany—"Look at the poor nigger on the wall. Look at him. Look at the poor nigger. Look at the poor nigger . . . on . . . the . . . wall. Fuck him . . . Fuck the nigger on the wall. Black man . . . is . . . de . . . debil?" (p. 233)—is only the most lyrical of Bateman's expressions of racism. African Americans, Chinese, Japanese, Iranians, Hispanics, Bateman hates them all. Why is he so often overcome with racial hatred, when his powerful position in society is unassailable? Does the novel participate in this racism, or put it at an effective satirical and critical distance? What is the relation between this racism and the text's humor?

How funny is American Psycho?

Think of the best comic scenes and gags in the novel: the confrontation in the Chinese dry cleaners; the business card showdown; Bateman's reversal of opinion on a pizza because Donald Trump liked it; the whole Luis Carruthers scenario; the condom farce with Courtenay; *The Patty Winters Show* featuring Bigfoot and a small Cheerio; the chapters on pop music; the urinal cake gag; the fact that Patrick's preferred sexual act with Evelyn is "foreclosure"; the pun on "murders and executions". Does *American Psycho* qualify as a properly comic novel (like, for instance, *Catch 22*)? Is its humor sufficiently broad to be considered acceptably funny? Or does its humour always stray onto the territory of the unacceptable, the taboo, the illicit? What is the relationship between laughter and the taboo?

Why can nobody tell anybody apart from anybody else?

More than a dozen names are applied to Patrick Bateman 'erroneously' during the novel. As he says, "I think a lot of snowflakes are alike . . . and I think a lot of people are alike too" (p. 378); ". . . everyone is interchangeable anyway" (p. 379). This is a consistent theme in Ellis's fiction. What sorts of effects and meanings are derived in this novel from the persistent confusion all the characters experience among themselves? Who is Paul Owen, Marcus Halberstram, Tim Price? Who is Patrick Bateman?

'. . . no one is safe, nothing is redeemed'

Why does Bateman go unpunished?

Sir Philip Sidney once proposed that literature was superior to philosophy because it made its arguments into concrete actions, and to history because in fiction the villains never get away with it. Patrick Bateman does. Much of the debate sparked by the initial publication of the book revolved around the apparent amorality of a work of literature which not only appeared not to condemn a killer's actions (because it presented them from his own point of view), but guaranteed that he would get away with murder by making the police and 'detective' risibly ineffectual. Is this fair? Does Patrick actually kill anyone after all? Or is there not something provocative and pointed in showing that the social class he represents very precisely *gets away with it*, all the time? What higher authority is there to judge and condemn Patrick today? How could that authority be represented in the novel?

Why does Bateman sometimes address us?

The second person pronoun occasionally appears: "Did I do this on purpose? What do you think? Or did I do this accidentally?" (p. 82); "By the time you finish reading this sentence, a Boeing jetliner will take off or land somewhere in the world" (p. 275); "There has been no reason for me to tell you any of this. This confession has meant *nothing.* . . ." (p. 377). What is the effect of this direct address to us? Is the whole book a 'confession'? Do we feel implicated and contaminated by our sudden proximity to this narrator, or is he somehow made safer and less intimidating by his appeals? More like us?

What are we to make of the literary references?

From Gertrude Stein ("a Rolls is a Rolls is a Rolls", p. 342) to Dostoevsky (the epigram from *Notes from the Underground*), Dante (the grafitto on Chemical Bank, p. 3), Hemingway, Pasternak (both mentioned on p. 280—*Farewell* is Bateman's "favorite Hemingway"), Tom Wolfe and Victor Hugo by default, there are many literary references scattered throughout the text (though not nearly as many as there are pop cultural references). What is the purpose of these? Do they help us to situate Ellis's concerns, or are the references usually ironic and satirical?

Why all the movie and television references?

Consider the following quotations:

". . . all of that fades and in what seems like time-lapse photography—but in slow motion, like a movie—the sun goes down, the city gets darker . . ." (p. 114); "I am so used to imagining everything happening the way it occurs in movies, visualizing things falling somehow into the shape of events on a screen, that I almost hear the swelling of an orchestra, can almost hallucinate the camera panning low around us, fireworks bursting in slow motion overhead, the seventy-millimeter image of her lips parting and the subsequent murmur of I *want* you in Dolby sound" (p. 265); ". . . footage from the film in my head is endless shots of stone and any language heard is utterly foreign, the sound flickering away over new images . . ." (p. 343); "Everything outside of this is like some movie I once saw" (p. 345); "guns flashing like in a movie" (p. 350), "like in some movie no one has heard anything, has any idea of what I'm talking about" (p. 367); and so on.

Bateman's psychology and perceptions are obviously predicated, to an extreme degree, on the technology, economics and spectacularity of film and television. Does this mean that, by and large, most of what he tells us is simply a vividly related version of a cinematic fantasy flickering through his own psyche? Is the point that Bateman's mind has been colonized and molded by film and television to the point that he can no longer distinguish between 'real' and 'imagined'? What is the status of literature in the age of the image? How can writers compete with such overpowering visual messages? Can we only describe mental functions by way of cinematic devices?

> Both Ellis and his central character seem to repudiate the premises of 'Realist' fiction: "Our lives are *not* all interconnected. That theory is a crock. . . . I have no patience . . . for events that take place beyond the realm of my immediate vision."

What is the significance of this?

Literary Realism, as practiced by Charles Dickens and George Eliot, and more importantly by Tom Wolfe in *The Bonfire of the Vanities*, depends upon the ideal of an 'omniscient narrator' who sees all, and is able through an act of narrative totalization to bring all the strands together into one compelling vision of the Whole. Ellis, through Bateman, condemns this approach. Why? What lessons are we to learn from the fact that Bateman refuses to see beyond his own terribly limited horizon? What does it tell us about the social group he represents? How are the perspectives of other groups represented in the novel? How would it be possible to combine Bateman's world view and the world view of Al "the bum" in one single, persuasive whole? Is Realism dead?

> "With the first three books [including *American Psycho*], narrative wasn't something I thought about or was particularly interested in. As a satirist I was more interested in milieu and behavior and skew-

ering the times I lived in and identifying certain attitudes that I
thought were prevalent in society." (Bret Easton Ellis)

Why doesn't American Psycho *tell a story?*

At least Jonathan Swift managed to combine his bilious satire with
a rollicking good adventure yarn in *Gulliver's Travels*, and if *Tristram Shandy* failed to tell a story, it was because the conventions
Lawrence Sterne was satirizing were precisely those of the narrative
novel. Ellis demotes 'narrative' to a very lowly status indeed in his
pursuit of satiric ends. Does this make the book better or worse?
Would a more convincing or enthralling story have boosted or
defanged the satire?

Does Bret Easton Ellis recapitulate Joan Didion's aesthetic to the point of falling foul of Tony Tanner's criticism of her novel Play It as It Lays*?*

"I would say that in its deep structure the book is almost completely
cliché-ic. It offers a species of instant supermarket nihilism. What
the words refer to is upsetting and disturbing enough. . . . But the
patterning of the words is ultimately undisturbing. . . . This is commodity nihilism which involves us in no new experience of negation, no real refusal of society, and in itself offers no evidence of
struggle against being a commodity. The test is not in what the
book appears to refer to . . . , but in what the book does to us as
readers. It sets us no tasks, it does not drive us back to our own
discourses to discover there the accumulating clichés and stereotypes which we mistake for thinking."[20] How much of a literary
radical is Ellis?

Is Bret Easton Ellis a conservative moralist in wolf's clothing?

Is Ellis nostalgic for a golden suburban past of patriarchal authority, two-door garages, and a belief in and fear of God? Or is he not rather nostalgic for a period of genuine youth revolt, bohemian and artistic dissidence, and a general proto-political resistance to the conformities and banalities of the present? Is it possible to decide between these two alternatives on the basis of this novel?

FURTHER READING

Here follows a list of titles that will both deepen and broaden one's appreciation of Ellis's achievement in *American Psycho*. A brief discussion of the list then follows.

Bret Easton Ellis, *Less Than Zero*
————,*The Rules of Attraction*
————,*The Informers*
————, *Glamorama*

Joan Didion, *Play It As It Lays*
————, *Slouching Towards Bethlehem*
————, *The White Album*

Tom Wolfe, *The Bonfire of the Vanities*

Ernest Hemingway, *The Sun Also Rises*

F. Scott Fitzgerald, *The Beautiful and the Damned*
————, *This Side of Paradise*
————, *The Crack-Up*

Dennis Cooper, *Frisk*
————, *Closer*

Jay McInerney, *Bright Lights, Big City*
———, *Brightness Falls*
———, *Story of My Life*

Tama Janowitz, *Slaves of New York*
———, *A Cannibal in Manhattan*

Lynne Tillman, *Haunted Houses*

Gary Indiana, *Rent Boy*
———, *Resentment*
———, *Gone Tomorrow*

Hubert Selby, Jr., *Last Exit to Brooklyn*
———, *The Demon*

Anyone who has been gripped by the style or milieu of *American Psycho* will want first of all to go further into the *ouevre* of Bret Easton Ellis, since as I suggested in the first chapter, his fictional universe constitutes a rather integrated experience for the reader. Characters familiar to you from one novel will reappear in others; and *Glamorama* even features a walk-on appearance by Patrick Bateman himself. (Ellis apparently could not resist an awful pun, as Bateman leans over a woman and tells her, "I like to keep abreast.") More importantly, the series of novels demonstrates a genuine thematic and tonal consistency, as Ellis has continued to explore the same territory with increasing formal sophistication throughout his career.

Clearly, however, these thematic concerns, and the style in which they are presented — flat, paratactic, affectless, monosyllabic, anti-'literary' — have both purchases in the literary past and amplifications in the present. First among Ellis's influences is Joan Didion, whose novel *Play It as It Lays* is the most important in coming to terms with Ellis's own preoccupations. Along with the essays collected in *Slouching Towards Bethlehem* and *The White Album*, this novel underscores the pivotal turn made by Didion in the 1960s, away from the complex postmodern stylistic games of Pynchon, Barthelme, Gaddis, and towards a refined, post-ideological style capable of 'objectifying' the present as a flat and hollowed-out space without past or future.

Tom Wolfe, another 'New Journalist', is also important in terms of Ellis's immediate concerns with *American Psycho*. *The Bonfire of the Vanities*, published two years prior to *American Psycho*, is concerned with much the same intellectual territory: the collapse of an ethical system in the full glare of materialism and consumerism in 1980s New York, the cool cynicism of the professional class, and so on. The central protagonist, Sherman McCoy, works for Pierce and Pierce investment bank (the same firm Patrick Bateman works for), but, unlike Bateman, is drawn into a series of disasters which precipitate his 'fall' from yuppie grace. Wolfe attempts in this novel to resuscitate the conventions and scope of the classic nineteenth-century 'Realist' novel, with the animating idea that fiction is capable of representing all the interconnecting social wheels of reality, from the lowest sphere to the highest circles. We have seen that Ellis proceeds from rather different aesthetic protocols, and on the contrary seeks to immerse himself utterly in the most blinkered, abstract and disengaged of all the social atoms available to him.

Meanwhile, looking backward in the American literary tradition, there are clear echoes in Ellis's work of two of the masters of American modernism, namely Ernest Hemingway and F. Scott Fitzgerald. Taking only the most representative moment in the short fiction of Hemingway, there is a clear affinity between the moral and stylistic universe of *American Psycho* and that famous moment in 'A Clean, Well-Lighted Place':

What did he fear? It was not fear or dread. It was a nothing that he knew too well. It was all a nothing and a man was nothing too. It was only that and light was all it needed and a certain cleanness and order. Some lived in it and never felt it but he knew it all was nada y pues nada y nada y pues nada. Our nada who art in nada, nada be thy name thy kingdom nada thy will be nada in nada as it is in nada.

And just as Bateman can squeeze no 'authenticity' out of life apart from deliriously imagined violence towards other human beings — reducing bodies to component parts the way he can disassemble his stereo system — so Jake Barnes, the narrator of *The Sun Also Rises*, can only find an escape from the insipid moral climate of his contemporaries through recourse to the archaic violence of the bull ring. And Scott Fitzgerald, though he was to produce no satire on the scale of *American Psycho*, was certainly attuned to the foibles and essential loneliness of his 'Jazz' generation, in something of the same way that Ellis is to his. Ellis is, however, more pessimistic that Fitzgerald, and to see where he derived this sort of pessimism, I recommend a reading of Hubert Selby Jr.'s bleak and powerful novel, *Last Exit to Brooklyn*.

It is perhaps this 'harder' vision which associates Ellis more with his own generation of writers than with any of the older authors. As a member of the 'Brat Pack' of eighties writers, Ellis brings with him a more cynical, disabused notion of the social than Fitzgerald could every have envisaged. I list only the more important of these contemporaries above, and particularly recommend the work of Ellis's good friend, the Los Angeles writer Dennis Cooper, who has also tried, albeit in a very different register, to use the allegories of violence and serial killing as a means of probing the most powerful and problematic contradictions in contemporary American consumer culture.

Notes

1. Ellis, interview with Jaime Clarke, at *http://www.geocities.com/Athens/Forum/8506/Ellis/clarkeint.html*. All other quotations from interviews in this chapter are taken from this, the best on record, which took place on two occasions, November 4, 1996 and October 22, 1998.

2. Selections available on *http://members.aol.com/_ht_a/tlmorganfield/articles/index.htm*.

3. Ellis, *The Informers*, p. 134.

4. Young, *Shopping in Space*, p. 120.

5. Elizabeth Young, *Shopping in Space*, p. 104.

6. Interview with Jaime Clarke, at *http://www.geocities.com/Athens/Forum/8506/Ellis/clarkeint.html*.

7. Young, op. cit., p. 115.

8. Interview with Eileen Battersby, *Irish Times*, Feb. 25, 1999.

9. Young, op. cit, p. 108.

10. *Rolling Stone*, April 1991.

11. Robert Fitch, *The Assassination of New York*, p. xii.

12. Ellis, interview with Jaime Clarke, at *http://www.geocities.com/Athens/Forum/8506/Ellis/clarkeint.html*.

13. "Vintage Buys Violent Book Dropped by Simon & Schuster", *New York Times*, Sunday, Nov. 17, 1990.

14. "NOW Chapter Seeks Boycott of "Psycho" Novel", *New York Times*, Thursday, Dec. 6, 1990.

15. *New York Times*, Sunday, Dec. 16, 1990

16. "Children of the Pied Piper", *Vanity Fair* (March 1991).

17. *The Guardian*, April 1991.

18. *Rolling Stone*, 4 April, 1991.

19. *The Onion* interview, *http://avclub.theonion.com/avclub3510/avfeature3510.html*

20. Tony Tanner, *Scenes of Nature, Signs of Men*, p. 182.

Bibliography

Works by Bret Easton Ellis

American Psycho. New York: Vintage, 1991; London: Picador, 1991.
Glamorama. New York: Alfred A. Knopf, 1998; London: Picador, 1999.
The Informers. New York: Alfred A. Knopf, 1994; London: Picador, 1994.
Less Than Zero. New York: Simon & Schuster, 1985; London: Picador, 1986.
The Rules of Attraction. New York: Simon & Schuster, 1987; London: Picador, 1988.

Select Criticism

Annesley, J. *Blank Fictions: Consumerism, Culture and the Contemporary American Novel*. London: Pluto, 1998.
Bowman, J. "*American Psycho*". *The Times Literary Supplement*. March 15, 1991: 12.
Cooper, D. "More than Zero". *Artforum*. 28: 7. 2000: 29–30.
Eberly, R. *Citizen Critics: Literary Public Spheres*. Urbana: University of Illinois Press, 2000.
Fitch, R. *The Assassination of New York*. London: Verso, 1993.

Freccero, C. "Historical Violence, Censorship and the Serial Killer—Bret Easton Ellis: The Case of *American Psycho*". *Diacritics—A Review of Contemporary Criticism.* 27: 2. 1997: 44–58.

Helyer, R. "Parodied to Death: The Postmodern Gothic of *American Psycho*". *Modern Fiction Studies.* 46: 3. 2000: 725–46.

Irving, J. "Is Pornography to Blame? Sexual Violence." *New York Times Book Review.* June 7, 1992: 34.

Smith, N. *The New Urban Frontier: Gentrification and the Revanchist City.* London: Routledge, 1996.

Tanner, T. *Scenes of Nature, Signs of Men.* Cambridge: Cambridge University Press, 1987.

Tucker, K. "The Splatterpunk Trend, and Welcome to It". *New York Times Book Review.* March 24, 1991: 13–14.

Young, E. and G. Caveney. *Shopping in Space: Essays on American 'Blank Generation' Fiction.* London: Serpent's Tail, 1992.

Websites

http://www.geocities.com/Athens/Forum/8506
http://www.altx.com/interviews/bret.easton.ellis.html
http://www.plastic.com/altculture/01/04/09/2158221.shtml
http://www.zip.com.au; sh~kylaw/TabulaRasa/Issue2/AmericanPsychoFiles.html
http://www.theavclub.com/avclub3510/avfeature3510.html
http://www.feedmag.com/96.08selzter/96.08seltzer.html
http://www.catharton.com/authors/52.htm